T5-BZG-221

PUTTING PEOPLE ON THE MAP

PROTECTING CONFIDENTIALITY WITH LINKED SOCIAL-SPATIAL DATA

Panel on Confidentiality Issues Arising from the Integration of
Remotely Sensed and Self-Identifying Data

Myron P. Gutmann and Paul C. Stern, Editors

Committee on the Human Dimensions of Global Change
Division of Behavioral and Social Sciences and Education

NATIONAL RESEARCH COUNCIL
OF THE NATIONAL ACADEMIES

THE NATIONAL ACADEMIES PRESS
Washington, D.C.
www.nap.edu

THE NATIONAL ACADEMIES PRESS • 500 FIFTH STREET, N.W. • Washington, DC 20001

NOTICE: The project that is the subject of this report was approved by the Governing Board of the National Research Council, whose members are drawn from the councils of the National Academy of Sciences, the National Academy of Engineering, and the Institute of Medicine. The members of the committee responsible for the report were chosen for their special competences and with regard for appropriate balance.

This study was supported by Contract/Grant Nos. BCS-0431863, NNH04PR35P, and N01-OD-4-2139, TO 131 between the National Academy of Sciences and the U.S. National Science Foundation, the U.S. National Aeronautics and Space Administration, and the U.S. Department of Health and Human Services, respectively. Any opinions, findings, conclusions, or recommendations expressed in this publication are those of the author(s) and do not necessarily reflect the views of the organizations or agencies that provided support for the project.

Library of Congress Cataloging-in-Publication Data

Putting people on the map : protecting confidentiality with linked social-spatial data / Panel on Confidentiality Issues Arising from the Integration of Remotely Sensed and Self-Identifying Data, Committee on the Human Dimensions of Global Change, Division of Behavioral and Social Sciences and Education.
    p. cm.
"National Research Council."
Includes bibliographical references.
    ISBN 978-0-309-10414-2 (pbk.) — ISBN 978-0-309-66831-6 (pdf) 1. Social sciences—Research—Moral and ethical aspects. 2. Confidential communications—Social surveys. 3. Spatial analysis (Statistics) 4. Privacy, Right of—United States. 5. Public records—Access control—United States. I. National Research Council (U.S.). Panel on Confidentiality Issues Arising from the Integration of Remotely Sensed and Self-Identifying Data. II. Title: Protecting confidentiality with linked social-spatial data.
H62.P953 2007
174'.93—dc22
                                    2006103005

Additional copies of this report are available from the National Academies Press, 500 Fifth Street, N.W., Lockbox 285, Washington, DC 20055; (800) 624-6242 or (202) 334-3313 (in the Washington metropolitan area); Internet http://www.nap.edu.

Printed in the United States of America.

Cover image: Tallinn, the capital city and main seaport of Estonia, is located on Estonia's north coast to the Gulf of Finland. Acquired on June 18, 2006, this scene covers an area of 35.6 × 37.5 km and is located at 59.5 degrees north latitude and 25 degrees east longitude. The red dots are arbitrarily selected and do not correspond to the locations of actual research participants.

Cover credit: NASA/GSFC/METI/ERSDAC/JAROS and U.S./Japan ASTER Science Team.

Suggested citation: National Research Council. (2007). *Putting People on the Map: Protecting Confidentiality with Linked Social-Spatial Data.* Panel on Confidentiality Issues Arising from the Integration of Remotely Sensed and Self-Identifying Data. M.P. Gutmann and P.C. Stern, Eds. Committee on the Human Dimensions of Global Change. Division of Behavioral and Social Sciences and Education. Washington, DC: The National Academies Press.

THE NATIONAL ACADEMIES
Advisers to the Nation on Science, Engineering, and Medicine

The **National Academy of Sciences** is a private, nonprofit, self-perpetuating society of distinguished scholars engaged in scientific and engineering research, dedicated to the furtherance of science and technology and to their use for the general welfare. Upon the authority of the charter granted to it by the Congress in 1863, the Academy has a mandate that requires it to advise the federal government on scientific and technical matters. Dr. Ralph J. Cicerone is president of the National Academy of Sciences.

The **National Academy of Engineering** was established in 1964, under the charter of the National Academy of Sciences, as a parallel organization of outstanding engineers. It is autonomous in its administration and in the selection of its members, sharing with the National Academy of Sciences the responsibility for advising the federal government. The National Academy of Engineering also sponsors engineering programs aimed at meeting national needs, encourages education and research, and recognizes the superior achievements of engineers. Dr. Wm. A. Wulf is president of the National Academy of Engineering.

The **Institute of Medicine** was established in 1970 by the National Academy of Sciences to secure the services of eminent members of appropriate professions in the examination of policy matters pertaining to the health of the public. The Institute acts under the responsibility given to the National Academy of Sciences by its congressional charter to be an adviser to the federal government and, upon its own initiative, to identify issues of medical care, research, and education. Dr. Harvey V. Fineberg is president of the Institute of Medicine.

The **National Research Council** was organized by the National Academy of Sciences in 1916 to associate the broad community of science and technology with the Academy's purposes of furthering knowledge and advising the federal government. Functioning in accordance with general policies determined by the Academy, the Council has become the principal operating agency of both the National Academy of Sciences and the National Academy of Engineering in providing services to the government, the public, and the scientific and engineering communities. The Council is administered jointly by both Academies and the Institute of Medicine. Dr. Ralph J. Cicerone and Dr. Wm. A. Wulf are chair and vice chair, respectively, of the National Research Council.

www.national-academies.org

PANEL ON CONFIDENTIALITY ISSUES ARISING FROM THE INTEGRATION OF REMOTELY SENSED AND SELF-IDENTIFYING DATA

MYRON P. GUTMANN, *Chair,* Inter-university Consortium for Political and Social Research, University of Michigan, Ann Arbor

MARC P. ARMSTRONG, Department of Geography, University of Iowa

DEBORAH BALK, School of Public Affairs, Baruch College, City University of New York

KATHLEEN O'NEILL GREEN, Alta Vista Company, Berkeley, CA

FELICE J. LEVINE, American Educational Research Association, Washington, DC

HARLAN J. ONSRUD, Department of Spatial Information Science and Engineering, University of Maine

JEROME P. REITER, Institute of Statistics and Decision Science, Duke University

RONALD R. RINDFUSS, Department of Sociology and the Carolina Population Center, University of North Carolina at Chapel Hill

PAUL C. STERN, *Study Director*
LINDA DEPUGH, *Administrative Assistant*

Preface

The main themes of this report—protecting the confidentiality of human research subjects in social science research and simultaneously ensuring that research data are used as widely and as frequently as possible—have been the subject of a number of National Research Council (NRC) publications over a considerable span of time. Beginning with *Sharing Research Data* (1985) and continuing with *Private Lives and Public Policies: Confidentiality and Accessibility of Government Statistics* (1993), *Protecting Participants and Facilitating Behavioral and Social Science Research* (2003), and, most recently, *Expanding Access to Research Data: Reconciling Risks and Opportunities* (2005), a series of reports has emphasized the value of expanded sharing and use of social science data while simultaneously protecting the interests (and especially the confidentiality) of human research subjects. This report draws from those earlier evaluations and analyzes the role played by a type of data infrequently discussed in those publications: data that explicitly identify a location associated with a research subject—home, work, school, doctor's office, or somewhere else.

The increased availability of spatial information, the increasing knowledge of how to perform sophisticated scientific analyses using it, and the growth of a body of science that makes use of these data and analyses to study important social, economic, environmental, spatial, and public health problems has led to an increase in the collection and preservation of these data and in the linkage of spatial and nonspatial information about the same research subjects. At the same time, questions have been raised about the best ways to increase the use of such data while preserving respondent confidentiality. The latter is important because analyses that make the most productive use of spatial information often require great accuracy and precision in that information: for example, if you want to know the route someone takes from home to the doctor's office, imprecision in one or the other degrades the analysis. Yet precise information about spatial location is almost perfectly identifying: if one knows where someone lives, one is likely to know the person's identity. That tension between the need for precision and the need to protect the confidentiality of research subjects is what motivates this study.

In this report, the Panel on Confidentiality Issues Arising from the Integration of Remotely Sensed and Self-Identifying Data recommends ways to find a successful balance between needs for precision and the protection of confidentiality. It considers both institutional and technical solutions and draws conclusions about each. In general, we find that institutional solutions are the most promising for the short term, though they need further development, while technical solutions have promise in the longer term and require further research.

As the report explains, the members of the panel chose in one signifi- cant way to broaden their mandate beyond the explicit target of "remotely sensed and self-identifying" data because working within the limitation of remotely sensed data restricted the problem domain in a way at odds with the world. From the perspective of confidentiality protection, when social science research data are linked with spatial information, it does not matter whether the geospatial locations are derived from remotely sensed imagery or from other means of determining location (GPS devices, for example). The issues raised by linking remotely sensed information are a special case within the larger category of spatially precise and accurate information. For that reason, the study considers all forms of spatial information as part of its mandate.

In framing the response to its charge, the panel drew heavily on existing reports, on published material, and on best practices in the field. The panel also commissioned papers and reports from experts; they were presented at a workshop held in December 2005 at the National Academies. Two of the papers are included as appendixes to this report. Biographical sketches of panel members and staff are also included at the end of this report.

This report could not have been completed successfully without the hard work of members of the NRC staff. Paul Stern served as study director for the panel and brought his usual skills in planning, organization, consen- sus building, and writing. Moreover, from a panel chair's perspective, he is a superb partner and collaborator. We also thank the members of the Committee on the Human Dimensions of Global Change, under whose auspices the panel was constituted, for their support.

The panel members and I also thank the participants in the Workshop on Confidentiality Issues in Linking Geographically Explicit and Self-Identifying Data. Their papers and presentations provided the members of the panel with a valuable body of information and interpretations, which contributed substantially to our formulation of both problems and solutions.

Rebecca Clark of the Demographic and Behavioral Sciences Branch of the National Institute of Child Health and Human Development has been a tireless supporter of many of the intellectual issues addressed by this study, both those that encourage the sharing of data and those that encourage the protection of confidentiality; and it was in good part her energy that led to the study's initiation. We gratefully acknowledge her efforts and the financial support of the National Institute of Child Health and Human Development, a part of the National Institutes of Health of the Department of Health and Human Services; the National Science Foundation; and the National Aeronautics and Space Administration.

Finally, I thank the members of the panel for their hard work and active engagement in the process of preparing this report. They are a lively group with a wide diversity of backgrounds and approaches to the use of spatial and social science data, who all brought a genuine concern for enhancing research, sharing data, and protecting confidentiality to the task that confronted us. National Research Council panels are expected to be interdisciplinary: that's the goal of constituting them to prepare reports such as this one. This particular panel was made up of individuals who were themselves interdisciplinary, and the breadth of their individual and group expertise made the process of completing the report especially rewarding. The panel's discussions aimed to find balance and consensus among these diverse individuals and their diverse perspectives. Writing the report was a group effort to which everyone contributed. I'm grateful for the hard work.

This report has been reviewed in draft form by individuals chosen for their diverse perspectives and technical expertise, in accordance with procedures approved by the Report Review Committee of the National Research Council. The purpose of this independent review is to provide candid and critical comments that assist the institution in making the published report as sound as possible and ensure that the report meets institutional standards for objectivity, evidence, and responsiveness to the study charge. The review comments and draft manuscript remain confidential to protect the integrity of the deliberative process.

We thank the following individuals for their participation in the review of the report: Joe S. Cecil, Division of Research, Federal Judicial Center, Washington, DC; Lawrence H. Cox, Research and Methodology, National Center for Health Statistics, Centers for Disease Control and Prevention, Hyattsville, MD; Glenn D. Deane, Department of Sociology, University at Albany; Jerome E. Dobson, Department of Geography, University of Kansas; George T. Duncan, Heinz School of Public Policy and Management, Carnegie Mellon University; Lawrence Gostin, Research and Academic Programs, Georgetown University Law Center, Washington, DC; Joseph C. Kvedar, Director's Office, Partners Telemedicine, Boston, MA; W. Christopher Lenhardt, Socioeconomic Data and Applications Center, Columbia University, Palisades, NY; Jean-Bernard Minster, Scripps Institution of Oceanography, University of California, La Jolla, CA; and Gerard Rushton, Department of Geography, The University of Iowa.

Although the reviewers listed above provided many constructive comments and suggestions, they were not asked to endorse the conclusions or recommendations nor did they see the final draft of the report before its release. The review of this report was overseen by Richard Kulka, Abt Associates, Durham, NC. Appointed by the National Research Council, he was responsible for making certain that an independent examination of this report was carried out in accordance with institutional procedures and that all review comments were carefully considered. Responsibility for the final content of this report rests entirely with the authoring panel and the institutions.

Myron P. Gutmann, *Chair*
Panel on Confidentiality Issues Arising from the
Integration of Remotely Sensed and Self-Identifying Data

Contents

Executive Summary   1

1   Linked Social-Spatial Data: Promises and Challenges   7

2   Legal, Ethical, and Statistical Issues in Protecting Confidentiality   26

3   Meeting the Challenges   42

4   The Tradeoff: Confidentiality Versus Access   59

References   71

Appendixes

A   Privacy for Research Data   *81*
      Robert Gellman
B   Ethical Issues Related to Linked Social-Spatial Data   123
      Felice J. Levine and Joan E. Sieber

Biographical Sketches for Panel Members and Staff   160

Executive Summary

Precise, accurate spatial data are contributing to a revolution in some fields of social science. Improved access to such data about individuals, groups, and organizations makes it possible for researchers to examine questions they could not otherwise explore, gain better understanding of human behavior in its physical and environmental contexts, and create benefits for society from the knowledge flows from new types of scientific research. However, to the extent that data are spatially precise, there is a corresponding increase in the risk of identification of the people or organizations to which the data apply. With identification comes a risk of various kinds of harm to those identified and the compromise of promises of confidentiality made to gain access to the data.

This report focuses on the opportunities and challenges that arise when accurate and precise spatial data on research participants, such as the locations of their homes or workplaces, are linked to personal information they have provided under promises of confidentiality. The availability of these data makes it possible to do valuable new kinds of research that links information about the external environment to the behavior and values of individuals. Among many possible examples, such research can explore how decisions about health care are made, how young people develop healthy lifestyles, and how resource-dependent families in poorer countries spend their time obtaining the energy and food that they need to survive. The linkage of spatial and social information, like the growing linkage of socioeconomic characteristics with biomarkers (biological data on individuals), has the potential to revolutionize social science and to significantly advance policy making.

While the availability of linked social-spatial data has great promise for research, the locational information makes it possible for a secondary user of the linked data to identify the participant and thus break the promise of confidentiality made when the social data were collected. Such a user could also discover additional information about the research participant, without asking for it, by linking to geographically coded information from other sources.

Open public access to linked social and high-resolution spatial data greatly increases the risk of breaches of confidentiality. At the same time, highly restrictive forms of data management and dissemination carry very high costs: by making it prohibitively difficult for researchers to gain access to data or by restricting or altering the data so much that they are no longer useful for answering many types of important scientific questions.

CONCLUSIONS

CONCLUSION 1: Recent advances in the availability of social-spatial data and the development of geographic information systems (GIS) and related techniques to manage and analyze those data give researchers important new ways to study important social, environmental, economic, and health policy issues and are worth further development.

CONCLUSION 2: The increasing use of linked social-spatial data has created significant uncertainties about the ability to protect the confidentiality promised to research participants. Knowledge is as yet inadequate concerning the conditions under which and the extent to which the availability of spatially explicit data about participants increases the risk of confidentiality breaches.

Various new technical procedures involving transforming data or creating synthetic datasets show promise for limiting the risk of identification while providing broader access and maintaining most of the scientific value of the data. However, these procedures have not been sufficiently studied to realistically determine their usefulness.

CONCLUSION 3: Recent research on technical approaches for reducing the risk of identification and breach of confidentiality has demonstrated promise for future success. At this time, however, no known technical strategy or combination of technical strategies for managing linked spatial-social data adequately resolves conflicts among the objectives of data linkage, open access, data quality, and confidentiality protection across datasets and data uses.

CONCLUSION 4: Because technical strategies will be not be sufficient in the foreseeable future for resolving the conflicting demands for data access, data quality, and confidentiality, institutional approaches will be required to balance those demands.

Institutional solutions involve establishing tiers of risk and access and developing data-sharing protocols that match the level of access to the risks and benefits of the planned research. Such protocols will require that the authority to decide about data access be allocated appropriately among primary researchers, data stewards, data users, institutional review boards (IRBs), and research sponsors and that those actors are very well informed about the benefits and risks of the data access policies they may be asked to approve.

We generally endorse the recommendations of the 2004 National Research Council report, *Protecting Participants and Facilitating Social and Behavioral Sciences Research*, and the 2005 report, *Expanding Access to Research Data: Reconciling Risks and Opportunities*, regarding restricted access to confidential data and unrestricted access to public-use data that have been modified so as to protect confidentiality, expanded data access (remotely and through licensing agreements), increased research on ways to address the competing claims of access and confidentiality, and related matters. Those reports, however, have not dealt in detail with the risks and tradeoffs that arise with data that link the information in social science research with spatial locations. Consequently, we offer eight recommendations to address those data.

RECOMMENDATIONS

Recommendation 1: Technical and Institutional Research

Federal agencies and other organizations that sponsor the collection and analysis of linked social-spatial data—or that support data that could provide added benefits with such linkage—should sponsor research into techniques and procedures for disseminating such data while protecting confidentiality and maintaining the usefulness of the data for social-spatial analysis. This research should include studies to adapt existing techniques from other fields, to understand how the publication of linked social-spatial data might increase disclosure risk, and to explore institutional mechanisms for disseminating linked data while protecting confidentiality and maintaining the usefulness of the data.

Recommendation 2: Education and Training

Faculty, researchers, and organizations involved in the continuing professional development of researchers should engage in the education of researchers in the ethical use of spatial data. Professional associations should participate by establishing and inculcating strong norms for the ethical use and sharing of linked social-spatial data.

Recommendation 3: Training in Ethical Issues

Training in ethical considerations needs to accompany all methodological training in the acquisition and use of data that include geographically explicit information on research participants.

Recommendation 4: Outreach by Professional Societies and Other Organizations

Research societies and other research organizations that use linked social-spatial data and that have established traditions of protection of the confidentiality of human research participants should engage in outreach to other research societies and organizations less conversant in research with issues of human participant protection to increase attention to these issues in the context of the use of personal, identifiable data.

Recommendation 5: Research Design

Primary researchers who intend to collect and use spatially explicit data should design their studies in ways that not only take into account the obligation to share data and the disclosure risks posed, but also provide confidentiality protection for human participants in the primary research as well as in secondary research use of the data. Although the reconciliation of these objectives is difficult, primary researchers should nevertheless assume a significant part of this burden.

Recommendation 6: Institutional Review Boards

Institutional Review Boards and their organizational sponsors should develop the expertise needed to make well-informed decisions that balance the objectives of data access, confidentiality, and quality in research projects that will collect or analyze linked social-spatial data.

Recommendation 7: Data Enclaves

Data enclaves deserve further development as a way to provide wider access to high-quality data while preserving confidentiality. This development should focus on the establishment of expanded place-based enclaves, "virtual enclaves," and meaningful penalties for misuse of enclaved data.

Recommendation 8: Licensing

Data stewards should develop licensing agreements to provide increased access to linked social-spatial datasets that include confidential information.

The promise of gaining important scientific knowledge through the availability of linked social-spatial data can only be fulfilled with careful attention by primary researchers, data stewards, data users, IRBs, and research sponsors to balancing the needs for data access, data quality, and confidentiality. Until technical solutions are available, that balancing must come through institutional mechanisms.

1

Linked Social-Spatial Data:
Promises and Challenges

Precise, accurate spatial data are contributing to a revolution in some fields of social science. Improved access to such data, combined with improved methods of analysis, is making possible deeper understanding of the relationships between people and their physical and social environments. Researchers are no longer limited to analyzing data provided by research participants about their personal characteristics and their views of the world; rather, it has become possible to link personal information to the exact locations of homes, workplaces, daily activities, and characteristics of the environment (e.g., water supplies). Those links allow researchers to understand much more about individual behavior and social interactions than previously, just as linking biomedical data (on genes, proteins, blood chemistry) to social data has helped researchers understand the progress of illness and health in relation to aspects of people's behavior. The potential for improved understanding of human activities at the individual, group, and higher levels by incorporating spatial information is only beginning to be unlocked.

Yet even as researchers are learning from new opportunities offered by precise spatial information, these data raise new challenges because they allow research participants to be identified and therefore threaten the promise of confidentiality made when collecting the social data to which spatial data are linked. Although the difficulties of ensuring access to data while preserving confidentiality have been addressed by previous National Research Council reports (1993, 2000, 2003, 2005a), those did not consider in detail the risks posed by data that link the information in social science research with spatial locations. This report directly addresses the tradeoffs between providing greater access to data and protecting research participants from breaches of confidentiality in the context of the unique capacity of spatial data to lead to the identification of individuals.

THE NEW WORLD OF LOCATIONAL DATA

The development of new data, approaches, spatial analysis tools, and data collection methods over the past several decades has revolutionized how researchers approach many questions. The availability of high-resolution satellite images of Earth, collected repeatedly over time, and of software for converting those images into digital information about specific locations, has made new methods of analysis possible. Along with more and improved satellite images, there are aerial images, global positioning systems (GPS) and other types of sensors—especially radio frequency identification (RFID) tags that can be used to track people worldwide—that allow the possibility of ubiquitous tracking of individuals and groups. The same technologies also permit enhanced research about business enterprises, for example, by providing tracking information for commercial vehicles or shipments of goods.

With the advent of GPS, the goal of real-time, continuous global coverage with an accuracy finer than 1 meter has been achieved, though some caveats, such as difficulty with indoor coverage, apply. Triangulation based on cellular telephone signal strength can be used to establish location on the order of 100 meters in many locations, and researchers are now developing techniques for mapping mobile locations at much higher resolutions (Borriello et al., 2005). Satellite remote sensing instruments have improved by more than an order of magnitude during the past two decades in several dimensions of resolution. Commercial remote sensing firms provide data with a sub-meter ground resolution. With the increasing availability of hyperspectral sensor systems (those that sense in hundreds of discrete spectral bands along the electromagnetic spectrum), the amount of geographic information being collected from satellites has increased at a staggering pace.

Terrestrial sensing systems are also increasing in quantity and capability. Low-cost solid-state imagers with GPS control are now widely deployed by private companies and scientific investigators. In addition, fixed sensor arrays (e.g., closed circuit television) are now used routinely in many locations to provide continuous coverage of events in their field of view. As computers continue to decrease in size and power consumption while also increasing in computing and storage capacity, inexpensive *in situ* sensor networks are able to record information that is transmitted over peer-to-peer networks and other types of radio communication technologies (Culler,

Estrin and Srivastava, 2004; Martinez, Hart, and Ong, 2004). These devices are now rather primitive, often sensing single types of information such as temperature or pressure, but their capabilities are increasing rapidly. Moreover, their space requirements are decreasing; some researchers now describe nanoscale computing and sensing devices (Geer, 2006).

These emerging technologies are being integrated with other developing streams of technology—such as RFID tags (Want, 2006) and wearable computers (Smailagic and Siewiorek, 2002)—that are location and context aware. Indeed, the ubiquity of these devices has caused some to assert that traditional sensing and processing systems will, in essence, disappear (Streitz and Nixon, 2005; Weiser, 1991). These technologies are creating significant concerns about threats to privacy, although few, if any, of these concerns relate to research uses of the technologies. Nevertheless, emerging technological capabilities are an important part of the context for the research use of locational data.

As these new tools and methods have become more widely available, researchers have begun to pursue a variety of studies that were previously difficult to accomplish. For example, analysis of health services once focused on access as a function of age, sex, race, income, occupation, education, and employment. It is now possible to examine how access and its effects on health are influenced by distances from home and work to health care providers, as well as the quality of the available transportation routes and modes (Williams, 1983; Entwisle et al., 1997; Parker, 1998; Kwan, 2003; Balk et al., 2004). Improved understanding of how these spatial phenomena interact with social ones can give a much clearer picture of the nature of access to health care than was previously possible.

Critical to research linking social and spatial data are the development and use of geographical information systems (GIS) that make it possible to tie data from different sources to points on the surface of the Earth. This connection has great importance because geographic coordinates are a unique and unchanging identification system. With GIS, data collected from participants in a social survey can be linked to the location of the respondents' residences, workplaces, or land holdings and thus can be analyzed in connection with data from other sources, such as satellite observations or administrative records that are tied to the same physical location. Such data linkage can reveal more information about research participants than can be known from either source alone. Such revelations can increase the fund of human knowledge, but they can also be seen by the individuals whose data are linked as an invasion of privacy or a violation of a pledge of confidentiality.

Increasingly sophisticated tools for spatial analysis involving, but going far beyond, the simple digitized maps of the early geographical information systems have also contributed to this revolution. Not only has commercial software made spatial data processing, visualization, and integration relatively accessible, but several packages (including freeware; e.g., Anselin, 2005; Anselin et al., 2006; Bivand, 2006; also see http://www.r-project.org/) also make multivariate spatial regression analysis much easier (e.g., Fotheringham et al., 2002). Moreover, standard statistical software packages, such as Stata and Matlab, now have much greater functionality to accommodate spatial analytic models, and SAS (another software package) and Stata have increased flexibility to accommodate complex design effects often associated with spatially linked data.

SCOPE OF WORK

In response to such challenges of providing wider access to data used for social-spatial analysis while maintaining confidentiality, the sponsors of this study asked the National Academies to address the scientific value of linking remotely sensed and "self-identifying" social science data that are often collected in social surveys, that is, data that allow specific individuals and their attributes to be identified. The Academies were further asked to

> discuss and evaluate tradeoffs involving data accessibility, confidentiality, and data quality; consider the legal issues raised by releasing remotely sensed data in forms linked to self-identifying data; assess the costs and benefits of different methods for addressing confidentiality in the dissemination of such data; and suggest appropriate models for addressing the issues raised by the combined needs for confidentiality and data access.

In carrying out our study, it became clear that limiting the study to remotely sensed data unnecessarily restricted the problem domain. When social science research data are linked with spatially precise and accurate information, it does not matter in terms of confidentiality issues whether the geospatial locations are derived from remotely sensed imagery or from other means of determining location, such as GPS devices or address-matching using GIS technology. The issues raised by linking remotely sensed information are a special case within the larger category of spatially precise and accurate information. For that reason, the committee considered as part of its mandate all forms of spatial information. We also considered all forms of data collected from research participants that might allow them to be identified, including personal information about individuals, which may or may not be sensitive if revealed to others, and information about specific businesses enterprises. For purposes of simplicity we call all this personal and enterprise information used for the research considered here "social data," and their merger with spatial information "social-spatial data."

This report focuses mainly on microdata, specifically, information about individuals, households, or businesses that participate in research studies or supply data for administrative records that have the potential to be shared with researchers outside the original group that produced the data. This focus is the result of the fact that such individual-, household-, or enterprise-level data are easily associated with precise locations. Microdata are especially important because spatial data can compromise confidentiality both by identifying respondents directly and by providing sensitive information that creates risk of harm if linked to identifying data. In addition, spatially precise information may sometimes be associated with small aggregates of individuals or businesses; and care is always needed when sharing data that have exact locations, for example, a cluster of persons or families living near each other.

This report provides guidance to agencies that sponsor data collection and research, to academic and nonacademic institutions and their institutional review boards (IRBs), to researchers who are collecting data, to institutions and individuals involved in the research enterprise (such as firms that contract to conduct surveys), and to those organizations charged with the long-term stewardship of data. It discusses the challenges they face in preserving confidentiality for linked social and spatial data, as well as ways that they can simultaneously honor their commitment to share their wealth of data and their commitment to preserve participant confidentiality. Although all these individuals and organizations involved in the research enterprise have somewhat different roles to play and somewhat different interests and concerns, we refer to them throughout this report as *data stewards*. This focus on the responsibilities of those who share data for analysis does not absolve others who have responsibility for the collected information from thinking about the risks associated with spatially explicit data. The report therefore also speaks to those who use linked social-spatial data, including researchers who analyze the data and editors who publish maps or other spatially explicit information that may reveal information that is problematic from a privacy perspective (e.g., Monmonnier, 2002; Armstrong and Ruggles, 2005; Rushton et al., 2006).

This study follows and builds on a series of previous National Research Council reports that address closely related issues, including: issues of data access (1985); the challenges of protecting privacy and reducing disclosure risk while maximizing access to quality, detailed data for informed analyses (1993, 2000, 2003, 2004b); and ethical considerations in using micro-level data, including linked data (2005a). The conclusions and recommendations of several of these earlier studies inform this report. These earlier reports and other studies (e.g., National Research Council, 1998; Jabine 1993; Melichar et al., 2002), have generally developed two themes, one emphasizing the need for data—especially microdata—to be shared among researchers, and the other the need to protect research participants. While the theme of expanding access to data has included data produced by both individual researchers and government agencies, it has generally emphasized the latter. In the closely related area of environmental data, the National Research Council (2001) emphasizes that publicly funded data are a public good and that the public is entitled to full and open access.

The consensus of this work is that secondary use of data for replication and new research is valuable and that both privately and publicly produced data should be shared. The most recent report on the subject (National Research Council, 2005a) presents a concise set of recommendations that encourage increased access to publicly produced data. At the same time, these reports and studies have also insisted on the protection of research participants, mostly in the broader context of protecting all human research subjects.

This report supports the conclusions of the prior work while exploring new ground. None of the earlier reports considered the potential for breaches of confidentiality posed by the increase in research using linked social-spatial data. The analyses and recommendations included in this report strive to expand the field to the new world of locational data.

The concerns addressed in this report are raised in the context of a broader recognition that vast amounts of data are available about most residents of the United States, that these data have been collected and collated without the explicit permission of their subjects, and that invasions of privacy take place frequently (O'Harrow 2005; Dobson and Fisher 2003; Goss 1995; Fisher and Dobson 2003; Sui 2005; Electronic Privacy Information Center [http://www.epic.org/pivacy/census], 2003). Huge commercial databases of financial transactions, court records, telephone records, health information, and other personal information have been established, in many cases without any meaningful request to the relevant individuals for release of that information. These databases are often linked and the results made available for a fee to purchasers in a system that has greatly diminished individuals' and businesses' control over information about themselves. These invasions or perceived invasions of privacy, however, are not a subject of this report. All datasets that include personal information, including those created for commercial as well as research purposes, whether or not they have spatial information and those that do not, are in need of comprehensive care to prevent breaches of confidentiality and invasions of privacy. Neither this report nor earlier reports deal with the kinds of information technology security required to prevent breaches or invasions, in the case of this report because there is nothing special for spatial data about the need for that security.

PRIVACY, CONFIDENTIALITY, IDENTIFICATION, AND HARM

To understand the dimensions of the confidentiality problem, it is important first to distinguish the concepts of privacy, confidentiality, identification, and harm (see Box 1-1). *Privacy* concerns the ability of individuals to control personal information that is not knowable from their public presentations of themselves (see Appendix A for a more detailed discussion of privacy and U.S. privacy law). When someone willingly provides information about himself or herself, it is not an invasion of privacy, especially if the person has been informed that it is acceptable to terminate the disclosure at any time. An invasion of privacy occurs when an agent obtains such information about a person without that person's agreement. An invasion of privacy is especially egregious when the person does not want the agent to have the information. An example is the acquisition and sale of the mobile telephone records of individuals without their permission (New York Times, 2006).

Confidentiality involves a promise given by an agent—a researcher in the cases of interest in this report—in exchange for information. Before a research activity begins, the researcher explains the purposes of the project, describes the benefits and harms that may affect the research participant and society more broadly, and obtains the consent of the participant to

---

BOX 1-1
Brief Definitions of Some Key Terms

Privacy concerns the ability of individuals to control personal information this is not knowable from their public presentations of themselves. An *invasion of privacy* occurs when an agent obtains such information about a person without that person's agreement.

Confidentiality in the research context involves an agreement in which a research participant makes personal information available to a researcher in an exchange for a promise to use that information only for specified purposes and not to reveal the participant's identity or any identifiable information to unauthorized third parties.

Identification of an individual in a database occurs when a third party learns the identity of the person whose attributes are described there. *Identification disclosure* risk is the likelihood of identification.

Harm is a negative consequence that affects a research participant because of a breach of confidentiality.

continue. This process is called "informed consent" (see National Research Council, 1993). The researcher then collects the information—through interview, behavioral observation, physical examination, collection of biological sample specimens, or requests for the information from a third party, such as a hospital or a government agency. In exchange, the researcher promises to use that information only for specified purposes (often limited to statistical analysis) and not to reveal the participant's identity or any identifiable information to unauthorized third parties. If promises of confidentiality are kept, a participant's privacy is protected in relation to the information given to the researchers. In academic and other research organizations, the process of obtaining informed consent and making confidentiality promises is part of normal research protocol: institutional review boards have guidelines that require agreements and protection of confidentiality and the ethical standards of research communities provide further support for confidentiality.

Identification is a key element in confidentiality promises. Confidentiality means that when researchers release any information—analyses, descriptions of the project, or databases that might be used by third parties—they promise that the identity of the participants will not be publicly revealed and cannot be inferred. Identification of an individual in a database occurs when a third party learns the identity of the person whose attributes are described there. Identification obviously increases the risk of breaches of confidentiality. *Identification disclosure risk* is sometimes quantified in terms of the likelihood of identification. In the context of this study, precise spatial information increases the risk of disclosure and thus the likelihood of identification.

It is important to note that it is not so much the information that is being protected, but the link of the information to the individual. For example, it is acceptable to describe a person's survey answers or characteristics so long as the identity of the participant is not revealed. The danger inherent in a breach of confidentiality is not only that private information about an individual might be revealed, but also that the successful conduct of research requires that there be no breaches of confidentiality: any such breach may significantly endanger future research by making potential research participants wary of sharing personal information. Including spatial data in a dataset with social data greatly increases the possibility of identification while at the same time being necessary for certain kinds of analysis.

Harm is a negative consequence that affects a survey respondent or other research participant, in the instances of interest in this study, because of a breach of confidentiality. Social science research can cause various kinds of harm (for example, legal, reputational, financial, or psychological) because information is revealed about a person that she or he does not wish others to know, such as financial liabilities or a criminal record. In exceptional cases, identification of a participant in social science research could put the person at risk of physical harm from a third party. In linking social and spatial data, the need to prevent breaches of confidentiality remains serious, even if no discernable harm is done to respondents, because even apparently harmless breaches violate the expectations of a trusting relationship and can also damage the reputation of the research enterprise.[1]

Thus, the challenge to the research community is to preserve confidentiality (and also to protect private information to the extent possible). This means that research participants must be protected from identification especially, but not only, when identification can harm them. Though the chance of a confidentiality breach is never zero, the risk of disclosure depends on the nature of the data. The separate risk of harm also depends on the nature of the data. In some instances, confidentiality is difficult to protect but the risk of harm to respondents is low (e.g., when the data include only information that is publicly available); in others, confidentiality may be easy to protect (e.g., because the data include few characteristics that might be used to identify someone), but the risk of harm may be high if identification occurs (because some of the recorded characteristics could, if known, endanger the well-being of the respondent). When precise locational data are included in or can be determined from a dataset, researchers face tougher challenges of protecting confidentiality and preventing identification.

OPPORTUNITIES AND CHALLENGES FOR RESEARCHERS

In response to the growing opportunities for knowledge about relationships between social and spatial phenomena on the part of researchers and policy makers, research funders—especially the National Institute of Child Health and Human Development [National Institutes of Health], the National Science Foundation, and the National Aeronautics and Space Administration—the sponsors of this study, have contributed substantial resources to the creation of linked social-spatial datasets (see Box 1-2). Such datasets cover parts of the United States (Arizona State University, 2006; University of Michigan, 2005a), Brazil (Moran, Brondizio, and VanWey, 2005; Indiana University, 2006), Ecuador (University of North Carolina, 2005), Thailand (Walsh et al., 2005; University of North Carolina, 2006), Nepal (University of Michigan, 2005b), and other countries. One outstanding example is research on the relationship among population, land use, and environment in the Nang Rang district of Thailand, described in Figure 1-1.

---

[1]For more on the distinction between risk and harm, see the Risk and Harm Report of the Social and Behavioral Sciences Working Group on Human Research Protections (http://www.aera.net/aera.old/humansubjects/risk-harm.pdf, accessed January 2007).

FIGURE 1-1 Confidentiality in Nang Rong, Thailand. The image is an aerial photo with simulated households identified and linked to their farm plots. At this resolution, it is impossible to prevent identification of households.

BOX 1-2
An Example of Social-Spatial Data

A good example of a social-spatial dataset comes from the Nang Rong study, begun in 1984. This project covers 51 villages in Nang Rong district, Northeast Thailand, an agricultural setting in the country's poorest region. The researchers who work on this project have collected data from all households in each village, including precise locations of dwelling units and agricultural parcels. Social network data link households along lines of kinship as well as economic assistance— who helps whom with agricultural tasks. The project team also follows migrants out to their most common destinations, including Bangkok and the country's Eastern

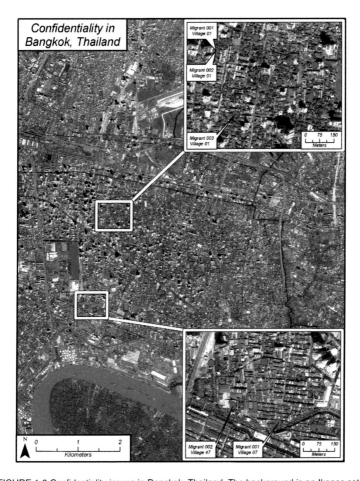

FIGURE 1-2 Confidentiality issues in Bangkok, Thailand. The background is an Ikonos satellite image, with simulated household data overlaid. The figure shows that migrants from the same village cluster at their destination, forming a village enclave (upper insert) or cluster with migrants from other Nang Rong villages forming a Nang Rong cluster (lower insert). Released in this fashion, the data can give away the identity of the migrants (unless circles are enlarged to cover more area in which case the quality of the data is degraded).

Seaboard—a government-sponsored development zone. The project's social data have been merged with the locations of homes, fields, and migration destinations, and then linked to a variety of other types of geographic information including satellite data, aerial photographs, elevation data, road networks, and hydrological features. These linked data have been used for many types of analysis (see University of North Carolina, 2006). Figures 1-1 and 1-2 are simulated data of the type created for the Nang Rong project. They show just how clearly individuals and households can be located in these data and therefore how easy it would be for anyone who has the spatial information for actual respondents to identify them.

Linking social data that are collected from individuals and households with spatial data about them, collected in place or by remote sensing, creates potential for improved understanding of a variety of social phenomena (see Butz and Torrey, 2006). Much has already been learned about the effects of context on social outcomes by analyzing social data at relatively imprecise geographic levels, such as census blocks and tracts or other primary sampling units (e.g., Gephart,1997; Smith and Waitzman 1997; Le Clere et al. 1998; Ross et al., 2000; Sampson et al., 2002). Advances in geographic information science and in remote sensing make it possible to connect individuals and households to their geographic and biophysical environments—and changes in them—at much finer scales.

Because concerns about confidentiality have limited the use of linked social and fine-scale spatial data, the potential for advancing knowledge through such linkages is only beginning to be explored. There are some early hints of exciting work, and we can speculate about future progress. Some of the progress involves studies of human interactions with the natural environment, a field that has been supported by the agencies that have requested the present study (e.g., National Research Council, 1998, 2005b). Researchers have combined household surveys with remotely sensed data on changes in land use to gain deeper understanding of the processes driving those changes and their economic consequences (e.g., conversion of agricultural land to urban uses, Seto, 2005; changes in cropping patterns, Walsh et al., 2005; changes in forest cover, Foster, 2005; Moran et al., 2005).

Another area of research and opportunity involves global population patterns. Global gridded population data demonstrates that people tend to live at low elevation and near sea coasts and rivers (Small and Cohen, 2004; Small and Nicholls, 2003) and that people living in coastal regions are disproportionately residents of urban areas. Moreover, coastal regions, whether urban or rural, are much more densely populated than other types of ecosystems (McGranahan et al., 2005). About one of every ten people on Earth lives in a low elevation coastal zone at risk of storm surges associated with expected increases in sea levels (McGranahan et al., 2006)

Interesting examples come from health research. For example, the availability of exercise options near where people live, including features as simple as a sidewalk, affects people's health and physical fitness (Gordon-Larsen et al., 2006). Other research shows how migration responds to local environmental conditions, with recurrent droughts perhaps providing the best example (Deane and Gutmann, 2003; Gutmann et al., 2006). There are opportunities for improving estimates of vulnerability to famine by combining data on food availability with data on household coping capabilities and strategies (Hutchinson, 1998). In one example, combining demographic survey data with environmental variables showed that household factors (composition, size, assets), maternal education, and soil fertility were all significant determinants of child hunger in Africa (Balk et al, 2005). The future of health research offers myriad opportunities. For example, environmental factors (e.g., air and water quality) have been linked to people's health: as social and biophysical datasets become better integrated at finer scales, it will be possible to examine a variety of environmental factors and link them to people's health with greater precision and so develop better understanding of those environmental factors.

Another example of the future of research concerns understanding travel behavior by linking personal data with fine-scale spatial information on actual travel patterns. Researchers could evaluate simultaneously the individual attributes of the research participants, the environmental attributes of the places they live, work, or otherwise frequent, and the detailed travel patterns that lead from one to another. Beyond knowing whether a route to school has a sidewalk and whether a child walks to school, one can ask whether that route also has a candy store or a community exercise facility and whether the actual trip to school allows the child to stop there. Yet combining all that information—location of home and school, route taken, and attributes of child and family—and publishing it would reveal the actual identities of research participants and so breach the promise of confidentiality made when data were collected from them.

As research combining spatial data with social data collected from individuals has expanded, both researchers and their sponsors have been forced to confront questions about the release of the massive amounts of data they have accumulated. The opportunities for research offer the potential for great benefits, but there is also some risk of harm. Moreover, both professional ethics and agency policies require that researchers share their data with others.[2] At the same time, researchers who collect social and behavioral data customarily promise the participants who provide the data confidentiality, and the same professional ethics and agency policies that require data sharing also require that pledges of confidentiality be honored. These requirements combine to produce the central dilemma that this report addresses.

---

[2]See, for example, the codes of ethics of the Urban and Regional Information Systems Association (http://www.urisa.org/about/ethics); the American Society of Photogrammetry and Remote Sensing (http://www.asprs.org/membership/certification/appendix_a.html); the American Sociological Association (http://www.asanet.org/galleries/default-file/Code%20of%20 Ethics.pdf) and the Association of American Geographers (http://www.aag.org/Publications/ EthicsStatement.html). Also see, for example, the policies of the National Institutes of Health (http://grants1.nih.gov/grants/guide/notice-files/NOT-OD-03-032.html) and the National Science Foundation (article 36 at http://nsf.gov/pubs/2001/gc101/gc101rev1.pdf). [All above-cited web pages accessed January 2007.]

In order to understand the challenges and opportunities, consider a recent finding and two hypothetical examples. The finding concerns the rapidly growing use of maps in medical research. Brownstein and colleagues (2006) identified 19 articles in five major medical journals in 2004 and 2005 that plotted the addresses of patients as dots or symbols on maps. To determine how easy it might be to identify individual patients from these maps, they created a simulated map of 550 geographically coded addresses of patients in Boston, using the minimum figure resolution required for publication in the *New England Journal of Medicine*, and attempted to reidentify the addresses using standard GIS technology. They precisely identified 79 percent of the addresses from the map, and came within 14 meters of precision with the rest. The authors' point was that improved ability to visualize disease patterns in space comes at a cost to patients' privacy.

The first hypothetical example concerns a researcher who (expanding on the insights in Gordon-Larsen et al., 2006) undertakes a project that includes a survey of adolescent behavior, including exercise and eating habits, in order to understand the causes of obesity in the teenage population. In addition to asking about how the research subjects get to school and the availability of places to walk and exercise, the researcher takes GPS readings of their homes and schools, and asks them to wear a device that tracks their location during waking hours for 1 week. Because of the complexity of the problem, the researcher asks about drug and alcohol consumption in addition to food consumption. Finally, the information obtained from the participants is merged with detailed maps of the communities in which they live in order to know the location of specific kinds of places and the routes between them. In the second example, a researcher interested in the effects of family size on land use and resource consumption in south Asia conducts a survey that asks each family about their reproductive and health history, as well as detailed questions about the ways that they obtain food and fuel. Then, walking in the community with family representatives, the researcher takes GPS readings of the locations of the families' farm plots and the areas where they gather wood for heat and cooking. Finally, the researcher spends a day with the women and children in the families as they go about gathering fuelwood, wearing a GPS-based tracking device so that the location and timing of their activities can be recorded. Some of these locations are outside the sanctioned areas in which the family is legally permitted to gather fuel.

In both hypothetical examples, the linking of the social data gathered from the participants and the spatial data will permit identification of some or all of the participants. Yet the researchers have made promises of confidentiality, which state that the data will only be analyzed by qualified researchers and that the participants will never be identified in any publication or presentation. Yet both the sponsor of the research and the research ethics require that the researchers make their data available to other researchers for replication and for new research. In both surveys, there are questions about activities that are outside officially sanctioned behavior, which if linked to an individual respondent might cause them harm if revealed.

In both hypothetical examples, the locational information is essential to the value of the data, so the researchers may not simply discard or modify data items that could lead to identification. Rather, they face a choice between honoring the requirement to share data and the commitment to protect confidentiality, or somehow finding a way to do both. Sharing data is not by itself automatically harmful to research participants. Responsible researchers regularly analyze data that include confidential information, and do so without compromising the promises that were made when the data were collected. The challenge arises when the data are shared with secondary researchers, who must either guarantee that they will adhere to the promise of confidentiality made by the original researcher, or receive data that are stripped of useful identifying information. The goal is to make sure that responsible secondary users do not reveal respondent identities, and do not share the data to others who might do so. But locational information may also make it possible for a secondary researcher to identify research participants by linking to data from other sources, without requesting permission for that information.

Some recent research suggests that it is possible to gauge social, demographic, and economic characteristics from remote sensing data alone (Cowen and Jensen 1998; Cowen et al 1993; Weeks, Larson, and Fugate, 2005), but this suggestive idea is unproven and would require considerable supporting research to overcome the challenge that the data are of limited value and have a high likelihood of error. Identifying social attributes from Earth-observing satellites is not easy, but satellite data, particularly from high-resolution satellites (launched since the late 1990s) make the identification of particular anthropogenic features—roads, buildings, infrastructure, vehicles—much easier than previously.[3] Other forms of spatial data, such as aerial photographs, especially historic ones, are much less likely to be accurately georeferenced (if georeferenced at all) for fine-scale matching with other attributes, but may nevertheless foster identification.

Spatial data create the possibility that confidentiality may be compromised indirectly by secondary data users in ways that identify individual participants.[4] Those ways relate to the spatial context of observations and the spatial covariance that exists among variables. Spatial covariance refers

---

[3]A review of satellites, their spatial and temporal resolutions and coverage, and detectable features can be found at http//sedac.ciesin.columbia.edu/tg/guide_frame.jsp?rd=RS&ds=1 [accessed January 2007].

[4]Confidentiality issues rarely, if ever, arise for spatial data when unlinked to social data. Much spatial data are in the public domain, and the Supreme Court has ruled that privacy rights do not exist for observations made from publicly navigable airspace (see Appendix A).

to the tendency of the magnitude of variables to be arranged systematically across space. For example, the locations of high values of one variable are often associated systematically with high values (or with low values) of another variable. Thus, if the spatial covariance structure between variables is known, and the value for one variable is also known, an estimate of the other variable can be made, along with an estimate of error. This knowledge can be applied in several ways, such as interpolation and contextual analyses associated with process models.

Interpolation methods can be placed into two classes: exact and approximate (Lam, 1983). Exact methods enforce the condition that the interpolated surface will pass through the observations. Approximate methods use the data points to fit a surface that may pass above or below the actual observations. Kriging is a widely used exact method in which the link between location (x,y) and value of the observation (z) is preserved. Kriging, therefore, threatens confidentiality because it exactly reproduces data values for each sample point: if the spatial location of sample data points is known, the linked values of other variables can be revealed (Cox, 2004). Kriging also provides the analyst with an assessment of the error at each point.

Contextual data are sometimes used to facilitate analysis when detailed exact data are either too sensitive for release or unavailable. However, contextual data can themselves be identifying; for example, a sequence of daily air quality monitoring readings from the nearest monitor provide a complete "signature" for each monitor, revealing fairly precise locations for individuals whose data are linked to such air quality readings. Knowledge about context can also be used to infer locations when deterministic spatial process models are used. Studies of the human effects of air pollution may use such models to study atmospheric dispersion of harmful substances. Given a model and a set of input parameters, such as wind speed, direction, temperature, and humidity, results are reported in the form of a plume "footprint" of dispersion (see, e.g., Chakraborty and Armstrong, 2001). If the location of a pollution source is known, along with the model and its parameters, a result from the model can be used to reveal the locations of participants in the dataset, who can then be identified, along with the confidential information they provided for the dataset.

DATA QUALITY, ACCESS, AND CONFIDENTIALITY: TRADEOFFS

More precise and accurate data are generally more useful for analysis. For analysis of social and spatial relationships, accuracy and precision in the spatial data are often crucial. However, having such data increases the chances that research participants can be identified, thus breaking researchers' promises of confidentiality. In general, as data with detailed locational information about participants becomes more widely accessible, the risk of a confidentiality breach increases. The problem of tradeoffs involving data quality, access, and confidentiality is becoming more urgent because of two recent trends. One is increased demands from research funders, particularly federal agencies, for improving data access so as to increase the scientific benefit derived from a relatively fixed investment in data collection. The other is the continuing improvement in computer technologies generally, and especially techniques for mining datasets—techniques that can be used not only to provide more detailed understanding of social phenomena, but also to identify research participants despite researchers' promises of confidentiality. The current context and a consideration of the ethical, legal, and statistical issues are discussed in Chapter 2.

This report also addresses ways to solve the problem of increasing the value of linked social-spatial data, both to the original researchers and to potential secondary users, while at the same time keeping promises of confidentiality to research participants. Chapter 3 examines several methods available for dealing with the problem. They can be roughly classified as technical and institutional, and each has significant limitations.

Both technical and institutional approaches limit the amount of data available, the usefulness of the data for research, or the ways that researchers can access those data in return for increased protection of pledges of confidentiality. Most researchers believe that those restrictions have had a negative effect on the amount and value of research that has been done, but there is relatively little solid evidence about the quantity of research *not performed* for this cause. It is not surprising that such negative evidence does not exist, and its absence does not prevent us from recommending improvements. At the workshop organized by the panel we heard testimony from users of data enclaves about the ways that the arduous rules of those institutions limited research. In addition, there was interesting testimony submitted at the time of the preparation of the 2000 U.S. census that documented research that could not be conducted because of variables and values that the Census Bureau proposed to remove from the Public Use Microdata Samples in order to reduce the risk of identification (Minnesota Population Center, 2000). The lack of readily accessible data about anything smaller than quite large areas does limit research. Research is not being done on certain topics that require knowledge of locations because the data are not available or access is difficult.

Some of the technical approaches involve changing data in various ways to protect confidentiality. One is to mask locations by shifting them randomly. This approach helps protect against identification, but makes the data less useful for understanding the spatial phenomena that justified creating the linked dataset in the first place—the significance of location of places (such as home and work) for the social conditions of interest. Researchers and data stewards need to be sensitive to linkages of data that are masked in order to avoid conclusions based on an overestimation of the accuracy of data that have been changed in some way.

Institutional approaches include restrictions in access to the data. The notion of tiers of access to data means that there is a gradient of accessibility: data that create the greatest risk of identification are least available and those with the lowest risk are the most available. At the same time, many analyses will only be possible with data that have the highest risk of disclosure and harm and therefore will be the least available.

The seriousness of these tradeoffs, in terms of the likelihood of identification or disclosure and of the potential for harm to research participants, depends on attributes of the research population, the information in the dataset, the contexts of inadvertent disclosure, and the motives of secondary users who may act as "data spies" (Armstrong et al., 1999) in relation to the dataset, as well as on the strategy used to protect confidentiality. Most of these factors apply regardless of whether the data include spatial information, but the availability of spatial characteristics of the research population can affect the seriousness of the tradeoffs. For example, a highly clustered sample of school-age students (with school as the primary sampling unit and with geographic identifiers) is more identifiable and more open to risk of harm than a nationally scattered sample of adults, especially if the data collected include information about social networks.[5] Many nonspatial factors can also affect disclosure risk. For example, questions about individuals' attitudes (what do you think about "x") are less likely to increase disclosure risk than questions about easily known characteristics of family or occupation (age, number of children, occupation, distance to place of employment).

At the same time, some questions, if identification occurs, are more likely to be harmful than others, with a question about drug use more likely to cause harm than a question about retirement planning. Finally, the seriousness of the tradeoffs may depend on the identities and motives of secondary users. At present, little is known about such users, what they might want, the conditions under which they might seek what they want from a confidential dataset, the extent to which what they want would lead to identification of research participants and their attributes, or the techniques that they might use (see, e.g., Duncan and Lambert, 1986b; Armstrong et al., 1999).

It is possible for the linkage of social and spatial data to create signifi-

---

[5]Because social networks locate individuals within a social space, releasing social network data involve analogous risks to the risks related to spatial network data discussed in this report. For discussions of ethical issues in social network research, see Borgatti and Molina (2003), Breiger (2005), Kadushin (2005), and Klovdahl (2005).

cant risks of harm to research participants. For example, it has been claimed that the Nazis used maps and tabulations of "Jews and Mixed Breeds" to round up people for concentration camps (Cox, 1996) and that the U.S. government used special tabulations of 1940 census data to locate Japanese Americans for internment (Anderson and Fienberg, 1997). Improvements in the precision of spatial data and advances in geocoding are likely to lower the costs of identifying people for such purposes. We note, however, that risks of identification and harm by governments or other organizations with strong capabilities for tracking people and mining datasets exist even if social data are not being collected under promises of confidentiality. The key issue for this study concerns the incremental risks of linking confidential social data to precise spatial information about research participants.

Among secondary users who might seek information about particular individuals, those who know that another person is likely or certain to be included in a database (e.g., a parent knowing that a child was studied or one spouse knowing about another) have a much easier time identifying a respondent than someone who starts without that knowledge. Experts suspect that although those who know which participant they are looking for may be interested in harming that individual, they are unlikely to be interested in harming the entire class of participants or the research process itself. The benefit-risk tradeoffs created by social-spatial is a major challenge for research policy.

2

Legal, Ethical, and Statistical Issues in Protecting Confidentiality

PAST AND CURRENT PRACTICE

There is a long tradition in government agencies and research institutions of maintaining the confidentiality of human research participants (e.g., de Wolf, 2003; National Research Council, 1993, 2000, 2005a). Most U.S. research organizations, whether in universities, commercial firms, or government agencies, have internal safeguards to help guide data collectors and data users in ethical and legal research practices. Some also have guidelines for the organizations responsible for preserving and disseminating data, data tables, or other compilations.

Government data stewardship agencies use a suite of tools to construct public-use datasets (micro and aggregates) and are guided by federal standards (Doyle et al., 2002; Confidentiality and Data Access Committee, 2000, 2002). For example, current practices that guide the U.S. Census Bureau require that geographic regions must contain at least 100,000 persons for micro data about them to be released (National Center for Health Statistics and Centers for Disease Control and Prevention, 2003). Most federal agencies that produce data for public use maintain disclosure review boards that are charged with the task of ensuring that the data made available to the public have minimal risk of identification and disclosure. Federal guidelines for data collected under the Health Insurance Portability and Accountability Act of 1996 (HIPAA) are less stringent: they prohibit release of data for regions with fewer than 20,000 persons. Table 2-1 shows the approaches of various federal agencies that regularly collect social data to maintaining confidentiality, including cell size restrictions and various procedural methods.

Fewer guidelines exist for nongovernmental data stewardship organizations. Many large organizations have their own internal standards and procedures for ensuring that confidentiality is not breached. Those procedures are designed to ensure that staff members are well trained to avoid disclosure risk and that data in their possession are subject to appropriate handling at every stage in the research, preservation, and dissemination cycle. The Inter-university Consortium for Political and Social Research (ICPSR) requires staff to certify annually that they will preserve confidentiality. It also has a continual process of reviewing and enhancing the training that its staff receives. Moreover, ICPSR requires that all data it acquires be subject to a careful examination that measures and, if necessary, reduces disclosure risk. ICPSR also stipulates that data that cannot be distributed publicly over the Internet be made available using a restricted approach (see Chapter 3). Other nongovernmental data stewardship organizations, such as the Roper Center (University of Connecticut), the Odum Institute (University of North Carolina), the Center for International Earth Science Information Network (CIESIN, at Columbia University), and the Murray Research Archive (Harvard University), have their own training and disclosure analysis procedures, which over time have been very effective; there have been no publicly acknowledged breaches of confidentiality involving the data handled by these organizations, and in private discussions with archive managers, we have learned of none that led to any known harm to research participants or legal action against data stewards.

Universities and other organizations that handle social data have guidelines and procedures for collecting and using data that are intended to protect confidentiality. Institutional review boards (IRBs) are central in specifying these rules. They can be effective partners with data stewardship organizations in creating approaches that reduce the likelihood of confidentiality breaches. The main activities of IRBs in the consideration of research occur before the research is conducted, to ensure that it follows ethical and legal standards. Although IRBs are mandated to do periodic continuing review of ongoing research, they generally get involved in any major way only reactively, when transgressions occur and are reported. Few IRBs are actively involved in questions about data sharing over the life of a research project, and fewer still have expertise in the new areas of linked social-spatial data discussed in this report.

Although not all research is explicitly subject to the regulations that require IRB review, most academic institutions now require IRB review for all human subjects research undertaken by their students, faculty, and staff. In the few cases for which IRB review is not required for research that links location to other human characteristics and survey responses, researchers undertaking such studies are still subject to standard codes of research ethics. In addition, many institutions require that their researchers, regard-

TABLE 2-1   Agency-Specific Features of Data Use Agreements and Licenses

Agency	Mechanisms for Data Approval*			
	IRB Approval Required	Institutional Concurrence	Security Pledges All Users	Report Disclosures
National Center for Education Statistics		X	X	X
National Science Foundation		X	X	X
Department of Justice	X	X	X	
Health Care Financing Administration				
Social Security Administration	X	X	X	X
Health Care Financing Administration-National Cancer Institute				
Bureau of Labor Statistics-National Longitudinal Survey of Youth			X	X
Bureau of Labor Statistics-Census of Fatal Occupational Injuries			X	X
National Institute of Child Health and Human Development	X	X	X	
National Heart, Lung, and Blood Institute	X			
National Institute of Mental Health	X	X		
National Institute on Drug Abuse	X	X		
National Institute on Alcohol Abuse and Alcoholism		X		

*The agreement mechanisms for data use range from those believed to be most stringent (IRB approval) on the left to the least stringent (notification of reports) on the right. In practice, policies for human subjects protection often comprise several mechanisms or facets of them. IRB approval and "institutional concurrence" are similar, though the latter often encompasses financial and legal requirements of grants not generally covered by IRBs.

less of their funding sources, undergo general human subjects protection training when such issues are pertinent to their work or their supervisory roles. IRBs are also taking a more public role; for example, making resources available for investigators and study subjects.[1] Educating IRBs and

[1]For example, see the website for Columbia University's IRB: http://www.columbia.edu/cu/irb/ [accessed April 2006].

Security Plan	Security Inspections	Cell Size Restrictions	Prior-approval Reports	Notification of Reports
X	X	X	X	X
X	X	X	X	X
	X		X	
		X		X
X	X		X	
X	X	X		X
X	X	X	X	
X	X	X		X
				X
				X
				X
				X

NOTE: Security plans may be quite broad, including safeguards on the computing environment as well as the physical security of computers on which confidential data are stored. Security inspections are randomly timed inspections to assess compliance of the security plan.

SOURCE: Seastrom (2002:290).

having IRBs do more to educate investigators may be important to increased awareness of confidentiality issues, but education alone does not address two challenges presented by the analysis of linked spatial and social data.

One of these challenges is that major sources of fine-grained spatial data, such as commercial firms and such government agencies as the National Aeronautics and Space Administration (NASA) and National Oceanic and Atmospheric Administration (NOAA), do not have the same history and tradition of the protection of human research subjects that are common in social science, social policy, and health agencies, particularly in relation to spatial data. As a result, they may be less sensitive than the National Institutes of Health (NIH) or the National Science Foundation (NSF) to the risks to research participants associated with spatial data and identification. Neither NASA nor NOAA has large-scale grant or research programs in the social sciences, where confidentiality issues usually arise. However, NASA and NOAA policies do comply with the U.S. Privacy Act of 1974, and in some research activities that involve human specimens or individuals (e.g., biomedical research in space flight) or establishments (such as research on the productivity of fisheries).[2] NASA and NOAA also provide clear guidance to their investigators on the protection of human subjects, including seeking IRB approval, obtaining consent from study subjects, and principal investigator education. For example, NASA's policy directive on the protection of human research subjects offers useful guidance for producers and users of linked spatial-social data, although it is clearly targeted at biomedical research associated with space flight.[3]

The difference in traditions between NASA and NOAA and other research agencies may be due in part to the fact that spatial data in and of themselves are not usually considered private. Although aerial photography can reveal potentially identifiable features of individuals and lead to harm, legal privacy protections do not apply to observations from navigable airspace (see Appendix A). Thus, agencies have not generally established human subjects protection policies for remotely sensed data. Privacy and confidentiality issues arise with these data mainly when they are linked to social data, a kind of linkage that has been regularly done only recently. These linkages, combined with dramatic increases in the resolution of images from earth-observing satellites and airborne cameras in the past decade, now make privacy and confidentiality serious issues for remote data providers. Thus, it is not surprising that NASA and NOAA are absent from the list of agencies in Table 2-1 that have been engaged in specifying data use agreements and licenses—another context in which confidentiality issues may arise. Agencies that already have such procedures established for social databases may be better prepared to adopt such procedures for spatial data than agencies that do not have established procedures for human subjects protection.

The other challenge is that, absent the availability of other information

---

[2]For details, see http://www.pifsc.noaa.gov/wpacfin/confident.php [accessed January 2007].
[3]See http://nodis3.gsfc.nasa.gov/npg_img/N_PD_7100_008D_/N_PD_7100_008D__main.pdf [accessed January 2007].

or expertise, IRBs have, for the most part, treated spatially linked or spatially explicit data no differently from other self-identifying data. There are no current standards or guidelines for methods to perturb or aggregate spatially explicit data other than those that exist for other types of self-identifying data. Current practice primarily includes techniques such as data aggregation, adding random noise to alter precise locations, and restricting data access. Without specialized approaches and specialized knowledge provided to IRBs, they can either be overly cautious and prevent valuable data from being made available for secondary use or insufficiently cautious and allow identifiable data to be released. Neither option addresses the fundamental issues.

The need for effective training in confidentiality-related research and ethics issues goes beyond the IRBs and investigators, and extends to data collectors, stewards, and users. Many professional organizations in the social sciences have ethics statements and programs (see Chapter 1 and Appendix B), and these statements generally require that students be trained explicitly in ethical research methods. Training programs funded by the NIH also require ethics components, but it is not at all certain that the coverage provided or required by these programs goes beyond general ethical issues to deeper consideration of ethics in social science research, let alone in the context of social-spatial linkages.[4] Professional data collection and stewardship organizations, as noted above, typically have mandatory standards and training. Nonetheless, there is no evidence that any of these organizations are systematically considering the issue of spatial data linked to survey or other social survey data in their training and certification processes. We offer some recommendations for improving this situation in Chapter 4.

LEGAL ISSUES

Researchers in college or university settings or supported by federal agencies are subject to the rules of those institutions, in particular, their Federalwide Assurances (FWAs) for the Protection of Human Subjects and the institutional review boards (IRBs) designated under their Assurances.

---

[4]For example, the Program Announcement for National Research Service Award Institutional Research Grants (T32) specifies: Although the NIH does not establish specific curricula or formal requirements, all programs are encouraged to consider instruction in the following areas: conflict of interest, responsible authorship, policies for handling misconduct, data management, data sharing, and policies regarding the use of human and animal subjects. Within the context of training in scientific integrity, it is also beneficial to discuss the relationship and the specific responsibilities of the institution and the graduate students or postdoctorates appointed to the program (see http://grants1.nih.gov/grants/guide/pa-files/PA-02-109.html [accessed April 2006]).

Also, researchers may find guidance in the federal statutes and codes that govern research confidentiality for various agencies.[5] Rules may also be defined legally through employer-employee or sponsor-recipient contracts. Obligations to follow IRB rules, policies, and procedures may be incorporated in the terms of such contracts in addition to any explicit language that may refer to the protection of human subjects.

Researchers who are not working in a college or university or who are not supported with federal funds may be bound, from a practical legal perspective, only by the privacy and confidentiality laws that are generally applicable in society. Such researchers in the United States usually include those working for private companies or consortia. In an international context, research may be done using human subjects data gathered in nations where different legal obligations apply to protecting privacy and confidentiality and where the social, legal, and institutional contexts are quite different. As a general rule, U.S. researchers are obligated to adhere to the laws of countries in which the data are collected, as well as those of the United States.

The notion of confidentiality is not highly developed in U.S. law.[6] Privacy, in contrast with confidentiality, is partly protected both by tort law concepts and by specific legislative protections. Appendix A provides a detailed review of U.S. privacy law as it applies to issues of privacy, confidentiality, and harm in relation to human research subjects. The appendix summarizes when information is sufficiently identifiable so that privacy rules apply, when the collection of personal information does and does not fall under privacy regulations, and what legal rules govern the disclosure of personal information. As Appendix A shows, the legal status of confidentiality is less well defined than that of privacy.

U.S. law provides little guidance for researchers and the holders of datasets except for the rules imposed by universities and research sponsors regarding methods by which researchers may gain access to enhanced and detailed social data linked to location data in ways that both meet their research needs and protect the rights of human subjects. Neither does current U.S. privacy law significantly proscribe or limit methods that might be used for data access or data mining. The most detailed provisions are in the Confidential Information Protection and Statistical Efficiency Act of 2002 (CIPSEA).[7] This situation makes it possible for researchers and organiza-

---

[5]An illustrative compendium of federal confidentiality statutes and codes can be found at http://www.hhs.gov/ohrp/nhrpac/documentsnhrpac15.pdf [accessed April 2006].

[6]For some references to federal laws on confidentiality, see http://www.hhs.gov/ohrp/nhrpac/documents/nhrpac15.pdf [accessed January 2007].

[7]E-Government Act of 2002, Pub. L. 107-347, Dec. 17, 2002, 116 Stat. 2899, 44 U.S.C. § 3501 note § 502(4).

tions that are unconstrained by the rules and requirements of universities and federal agencies to legally access vast depositories of commercial data on the everyday happenings, transactions, and movements of individuals and to use increasingly sophisticated data mining technology to conduct detailed analyses on millions of individuals and households without their knowledge or explicit consent.

These privacy issues are not directly relevant to the conduct of social science research under conventional guarantees of confidentiality. However, they may become linked in the future, either because researchers may begin to use these data sources or because privacy concerns raised by uses of large commercial databases may lead to pressures to constrain research uses of linked social and spatial data. Solutions to the tradeoffs among data quality, access, and confidentiality must be considered in the context of the legal vagueness surrounding the confidentiality concept and the effects it may have on individuals' willingness to provide information to researchers under promises of confidentiality.

ETHICAL ISSUES

The topics of study, the populations being examined, and the method or methods involved in an inquiry interact to shape ethical considerations in the conduct of *all* research involving human participants (Levine and Skedsvold, 2006). Linked social-spatial research raises many of the typical issues of sound science and sound ethics, for which the basic ethical principles have been well articulated in the codes of ethics of scientific societies,[8] in research and writing on research ethics, in the evolution of the Code of Federal Regulations for the Protection of Human Subjects (45 CFR 46) and the literature that surrounds it, and in a succession of important reports and recommendations typically led by the research community (see Appendix B). Much useful ethical guidance can also be extrapolated from past National Research Council reports (e.g., 1985, 1993, 2004b, 2005a).

In addition, as noted above, linked social and spatial data raise particularly challenging ethical issues because the very spatial precision of these data is their virtue, and, thus, aggregating or masking spatial identifiers to protect confidentiality can greatly reduce their scientific value and utility. Therefore, if precise spatial coordinates are to be used as research data, primary researchers and data stewards need to address how ethically to store, use, analyze, and share those data. Appendix B provides a detailed discussion of ethical issues at each stage of the research process, from primary data collection to secondary use.

---

[8]For example, see those of the American Statistical Association, at http://www.amstat.org/profession/index.cfm?fuseaction=ethicalstatistics [accessed January 2007].

The process of linking micro-level social and spatial data is usually considered to fall in the domain of human subjects research because it involves interaction or intervention with individuals or the use of identifiable private information.[9] Typically, such research is held to ethical guidelines and review processes associated with IRBs at colleges, universities, and other research institutions. This is the case whether or not the research is funded by one of the federal agencies that are signatories to the federal regulations on human subjects research.[10] Thus, generic legal and ethical principles for data collection and access apply. Also, secondary analysts of data, including those engaged in data linking, have the ethical obligation to honor agreements made to research participants as part of the initial data collection. However, the practices of IRBs for reviewing proposed secondary data analyses vary across institutions, which may require review of proposals for secondary data analysis or defer authority to third-party data providers that have protocols for approving use.[11] Data stewardship—the practices of providing or restricting the access of secondary analysts to original or transformed data—entails similar ethical obligations.

Planning for ethically responsible research is a matter of professional obligation for researchers and other professionals, covered in part by IRBs under the framework of a national regulatory regime. This regime provides for a distributed human subjects protection system that allows each IRB to tailor its work with considerable discretion to meet the needs of researchers and the research communities in which the work is taking place. The linking of social and spatial data raises new and difficult issues for researchers and IRBs to consider: because the uses of linked data are to some extent unpredictable, decisions about data access are rarely guided by an explicit set of instructions.

The National Commission for the Protection of Human Subjects of Biomedical and Behavioral Research (1979) concisely conveyed the essential ethical principles for research:

---

[9]These are the elements of human subject research as defined in the Code of Federal Regulations at 45 CFR 46.102(f).

[10]Academic and research institutions typically have in place federally approved Federal-wide Assurances that extend the Federal Regulations for the Protection of Human Subjects to all human subjects research undertaken at the institution, not just to research funded by the 17 agencies that have adopted the Federal Regulations.

[11]IRBs even vary in whether research using public-use data files is reviewed, although increasingly the use of such data, if not linked to or supplemented by other data, is viewed as exempt once vetted for public use). See http://www.hhs.gov/ohrp/nhrpac/documents/dataltr.pdf for general guidelines and http://info.gradsch.wisc.edu/research/compliance/humansubjects/7.existingdata.htm for a specific example. [Web pages accessed January 2007].

Beneficence—maximizing good outcomes for society, science, and individual research participants while avoiding or minimizing unnecessary risk or harm;

respect for persons—protecting the autonomy of research participants through voluntary, informed consent and by assuring privacy and confidentiality); and

justice—ensuring reasonable, carefully considered procedures and a fair distribution of costs and benefits.

These three principles together provide a framework for both facilitating social and spatial research and doing so in an ethically responsible and sensitive way.

For primary researchers, secondary analysts, and data stewards, the major ethical issues concern the sensitivity of the topics of research; maintaining confidentiality and obtaining informed consent; considerations of benefits to society and to research participants; and risk and risk reduction, particularly the obligation to reduce disclosure risk. Linking spatial data to social data does not alter ethical obligations, but it may pose additional challenges.

Data collectors, stewards, and analysts have a high burden with regard to linked social and spatially precise data to ensure that the probability of disclosure approaches zero and that the data are very securely protected. They also need to avoid inadvertent disclosure through the ways findings are presented, discussed, or displayed. To meet this burden, they need to consider all available technical methods and data management strategies. We examine these methods and strategies in Chapter 3 in relation to their ability to meet the serious challenges of data protection for linked social-spatial data.

STATISTICAL ISSUES

All policies about access to linked social-spatial data implicitly involve tradeoffs between the costs and benefits of providing some form of access to the data, or modified versions of the data, by secondary data users. The risk of disclosures of sensitive information constitutes the primary cost, and the knowledge generated from the data represents the primary benefit. At one extreme, data can be released as is, with identifiers such as precise geocodes intact. This policy offers maximum benefit at a maximum cost (i.e., minimum confidentiality protection). At the other extreme, data can be completely restricted for secondary use, a policy that provides minimal benefit and minimal cost (i.e., maximum confidentiality protection). Most current methods of data release, such as altering or restricting access to the original data, have costs and benefits between these two extremes.

Well-informed data access policies reflect wise decisions about the tradeoffs, such as whether the data usefulness is high enough for the disclosure risks associated with a particular policy. However, most data stewards do not directly measure the inputs to these cost-benefit analyses. This is not negligence on the part of data stewards; indeed, the broader research community has not yet developed the tools needed to make such assessments. Yet, data stewards could quantify some aspects of the cost-benefit tradeoff, namely, disclosure risks and data quality. Evaluating these measures can enable data stewards to choose policies with better risk-quality profiles (e.g., between two policies with the same disclosure risk, to select the one with higher data quality). There have been a few efforts to formalize the task of assessing data quality and disclosure risk together for the purpose of evaluating the tradeoffs (Duncan et al., 2001; Gomatam et al., 2005). This section briefly reviews statistical approaches to gauging the risk-quality tradeoffs both generally and for spatial data. (For further discussion about the cost-benefit approach to data dissemination, see Abowd and Lane, 2003).

Most data stewards seeking to protect data confidentiality are concerned with two types of disclosures. One is identity disclosure, which occurs when a user of the data correctly identifies individual records using the released data. The other is attribute disclosure, which occurs when a data user learns the values of sensitive variables for individual records in the dataset. Attribute disclosures typically require identification disclosures (Duncan and Lambert, 1986a). Other types of disclosures include perceived identity disclosure, which occurs when a data user incorrectly identifies individual records in the database, and inferential disclosure, which occurs when a data user can accurately predict sensitive attributes in the dataset using the released data that may have been altered—for example, by adding statistical noise—to prevent disclosure. (For introductions to disclosure risks, see Federal Committee on Statistical Methodology, 1994; Duncan and Lambert, 1986a, 1986b; Lambert, 1993: Willenborg and de Waal, 1996, 2001.)

Efforts to quantify identity disclosure risk generally fall in two broad categories: (1) estimating the number of records in the released data that are unique records in the population and can therefore be at high risk of identification, and (2) estimating the probabilities that users of the released data can determine the identities of the records in the released data by using the information in those data. Although these approaches are appropriate for many varieties of data, in cases where there are exact spatial identifiers, virtually every individual is unique, so the disclosure risk is very great.

Quantifying Disclosure Risks

Methods of estimating the risk of identification disclosure involve estimating population uniqueness and probabilities of identification. Estimates of attribute disclosures involve measuring the difference between estimates of sensitive attributes made by secondary data users and the actual values. This section describes methods that are generally applicable for geographic identification at scales larger than that characterized by exact latitude and longitude (such as census blocks or tracts, minor civil divisions, or counties). In many cases, exact latitude and longitude uniquely identifies respondents, although there are exceptions (e.g., when spatial identifiers locate a residence in a large, high-rise apartment building).

Population uniqueness is relevant for identity disclosures because unique records are at higher risk of identification than non-unique records. For any unperturbed, released record that is unique in the population, a secondary user who knows that target record's correct identifying variables can identify it with probability 1.0. For any unperturbed released population non-unique target record, secondary users who know its correct identifying variables can identify that record only with probability $1/K$, where K is the number of records in the population whose characteristics match the target record. For purposes of disclosure risk assessment, population uniqueness is not a fixed quality; it depends on what released information is known by the secondary data user. For example, most individuals are uniquely identified in populations by the combination of their age, sex, and street address. When a data user knows these identifying variables and they are released on a file, most records are population unique records. However, when the secondary user knows only age, sex, and state of residence, most records will not be unique records. Hence, all methods based on population uniqueness depend on assumptions about what information is available to secondary data users. The number of population unique records in a sample typically is not known and must be estimated by the data disseminator. Methods for making such estimates have been reported by several researchers (see, e.g., Bethlehem et al., 1990; Greenberg and Zayatz, 1992; Skinner, 1992; Skinner et al., 1994; Chen and Keller-McNulty, 1998; Fienberg and Makov, 1998; Samuels, 1998; Pannekoek, 1999; Dale and Elliot, 2001.) These methods involve sophisticated statistical modeling.

Probabilities of identification are readily interpreted as measures of identity disclosure risk: the larger the probability, the greater the risk. Data disseminators determine their own thresholds for probabilities considered unsafe. There are two main approaches to estimating these probabilities. The first is to match records in the file being considered for release with records from external databases that a secondary user plausibly would use to attempt an identification (Paass, 1988; Blien et al., 1992; Federal Committee on Statistical Methodology, 1994; Yancey et al., 2002). The matching is done using record linkage software, which (1) searches for the records in the external data file that look as similar as possible to the records in the file being considered for release; (2) computes the probabilities that these matching records correspond to records in the file being considered for release, based on the degrees of similarity between the matches and their targets; and (3) declares the matches with probabilities exceeding a specified threshold as identifications.

The second approach is to match records in a file being considered for release with the records from the original, unperturbed data file (Spruill, 1982; Duncan and Lambert 1986a, 1986b; Lambert, 1993; Fienberg et al. 1997; Skinner and Elliot, 2002; Reiter, 2005a). This approach can be easier and less expensive to implement than obtaining external data files and record linkage software. It allows a data disseminator to evaluate the identification risks when a secondary user knows the identities of some or all of the sampled records but does not know the location of those records in the file being considered for release. This approach can be modified to work under the assumption that the secondary user does not know the identities of the sampled records.

Many data disseminators focus on identity disclosures and pay less attention to attribute disclosures. In part, this is because attribute disclosures are usually preceded by identity disclosures. For example, when original values of attributes are released, a secondary data user who correctly identifies a record learns the attribute values. Many data disseminators therefore fold the quantification of attribute disclosure risks into the measurement of identification disclosure risks. When attribute values are altered before release, attribute risks change to inferential disclosure risks. There are no standard approaches to quantifying inferential disclosure risks. Lambert (1993) provides a useful framework that involves specifying a secondary user's estimator(s) of the unknown attribute values—such as an average of plausible matches' released attribute values—and a loss function for incorrect guesses, such as the Euclidean or statistical distance between the estimate and the true value of the attribute. A data disseminator can then evaluate whether the overall value of the loss function—the distance between the secondary user's proposed estimates and the actual values—is large enough to be deemed safe. (For examples of the assessment of attribute and inferential disclosure risks, see Gomatam et al., 2005; Reiter, 2005d.)

The loss-function approach extends to quantifying overall potential harm in a data release (Lambert, 1993). Specifically, data disseminators can specify cost functions for all types of disclosures, including perceived identification and inferential disclosures, and combine them with the appropriate probabilities of each to determine the expected cost of releasing the data. When coupled with measurements of data quality, this approach provides a decision-theoretic framework for selecting disclosure limitation policies. Lambert's total harm model is primarily theoretical and has not been implemented in practice.

Quantifying Data Quality

Compared with the effort that has gone into developing measures of disclosure risks, there has been less work on developing measures of data quality. Existing quality measures are of two types: (1) comparisons of broad differences between the original and released data, and (2) comparisons of differences in specific models between the original and released data. The former measures suffer from not being tied to how users analyze the data; the latter measures suffer from capturing only certain dimensions of data quality.

Broad difference measures essentially quantify differences between the distributions of the data values on the original and released files. As the differences between the distributions grow, the overall quality of the released data drops. Computing differences in distributions is a nontrivial statistical problem, particularly when there are many variables and records with unknown distributional shapes. Most approaches are therefore ad hoc. For example, some researchers suggest computing a weighted average of the differences in the means, variances, and correlations in the original and released data, where the weights indicate the relative importance that those quantities are similar in the released and observed files (Domingo-Ferrer and Torra, 2001; Yancey et al., 2002). Such ad hoc methods are only tangentially tied to the statistical analyses being done by data users. For example, a user interested in analyzing incomes may not care that means are preserved when the tails of the distribution are distorted, because the researcher's question concerns only the extremely rich. In environmental research, the main concern may be with the few people with the greatest exposure to an environmental hazard. These measures also have limited interpretability and little theoretical basis.

Comparison of specific models is often done informally. For example, data disseminators look at the similarity of point estimates and standard errors of regression coefficients after fitting the same regression on the original data and on the data proposed for release. If the results are considered close—for example, the confidence intervals for the coefficients obtained from the models largely overlap—the released data have high quality for that particular analysis. Such measures are closely tied to how the data are used, but they only reflect certain dimensions of the overall quality of the released data. It is prudent to examine models that represent the wide range of expected uses of the released data, even though unexpected uses may arise for the conclusions of such models that do not apply.

A significant issue for assessing data quality with linked spatial-social data is the need at times to simultaneously preserve several characteristics or spatial relationships. Consider, for example, a collection of observations represented as points that define nodes in a transportation network, when a node is defined as a street intersection. Although it is possible to create a synthetic or transformed network that has the same mean (global) link length as the original one, it is difficult to maintain, in addition, actual variation in the local topology of links (the number of links that connect at a node), as well as the geographical variability in link lengths that might be present in the original data. Consequently, some types of analyses done with transformed or synthetic data may yield results similar to those that would result with the original data, while others may create substantial risks of inferential error. The results may include both Type I errors, in which a null hypothesis is incorrectly rejected, and Type II errors, when a null hypothesis is incorrectly accepted. Data users may be tempted to treat transformed data as equal quality to the original data unless they are informed otherwise.

Effects of Spatial Identifiers

The presence of precise spatial identifiers can have large effects on the risk-quality tradeoffs. Releasing these identifiers can raise the risks of identification to extremely high levels. To reduce these risks, data stewards may perturb the spatial identifiers if they plan to release some version of the original data for open access—but doing this can very seriously degrade the quality of the data for analyses that use the spatial information, and particularly for analyses that depend on patterns of spatial covariance, such as distances or topological relationships between research participants and locations important to the analysis (Armstrong et al., 1999). For example, some analyses may be impossible to do with coarsened identifiers, and others may produce misleading results due to altered relationships between the attributes and spatial variables. Furthermore, if spatial identifiers are used as matching variables for linking datasets, altering them can lead to matching errors, which, when numerous, may seriously degrade analyses.

Perturbing the spatial information may not reduce disclosure risks sufficiently to maintain confidentiality, especially when the released data include other information that is known by a secondary data user. For example, there may be only one person of a certain sex, age, race, and marital status in a particular county, and this information may be readily available for the county, so that coarsening geographies to the county level would provide no greater protection for that person than releasing the exact address.

Identity disclosure risks are complicated to measure when the data are set up to be meaningfully linked to other datasets for research purposes. Altering spatial identifiers will reduce disclosure risks in the set of data originally collected, but the risks may increase when this dataset is linked to datasets with other attributes. For example, unaltered attributes in File A may be insufficient to identify individuals if the spatial identifiers are altered, but when File A is linked to File B, the combined attributes and altered spatial identifiers may uniquely identify many individuals. The complication arises because the steward of the collected data may not know which attributes are in the files to be linked to those data, so that it is difficult to evaluate the degree of disclosure risk.

Even when safeguards have been established for data sharing, publication of research papers using linked social-spatial data may pose other problems such as those associated with the visualization of data. VanWey et al. (2005) present a means for evaluating the risks associated with displaying data through maps that may be presented orally or in writing to communicate research results. The method involves identifying data with a spatial area of a radius sufficient to include, on average, enough research participants to reduce the identity disclosure risk to a target value. Methods for limiting disclosure risk from maps are only beginning to be developed. No guidelines currently exist for visualizing linked social-spatial data, in published papers or even presentations; but future standards for training and publication contexts should be based on systematic assessment of such risks.

In principle, policies for access to data that include spatial identifiers can be improved by evaluating the tradeoff between disclosure risks and data quality. In practice, though, such an evaluation will be challenging for many data stewards and for IRBs that are considering proposals to use linked data. Existing approaches to quantifying risk and quality are technically demanding and may be beyond the capabilities of some data stewards. Low-cost, readily available methods for estimating risks and quality do not yet exist, whether or not the data include spatial identifiers. And existing techniques do not account for the additional risks associated with linked datasets. This challenge would be significantly lessened, and data dissemination practice improved, if data stewards had access to reliable, valid, off-the-shelf software and protocols for assessing the tradeoffs between disclosure risk and data quality and for undertaking broad cost-benefit analyses. The next chapter addresses the issue of evaluating and addressing the tradeoffs involving disclosure risk and data quality.

3

Meeting the Challenges

Although the challenges described in Chapter 2 are substantial, a number of possible approaches exist for preserving respondent confidentiality when links to geospatial information could engender breaches. They fall in two main categories: institutional approaches, which involve restricting access to sensitive data; and technical and statistical approaches, which involve transforming the data in various ways to enhance the protection of confidentiality. This chapter describes these two broad categories of approaches.

INSTITUTIONAL APPROACHES

Institutions that have responsibility for preserving the confidentiality of respondents employ a number of strategies. These strategies are very important for protecting respondent confidentiality in survey data under all circumstances, and especially when there is a high risk of identification due to the existence of precise geospatial attributes. At their heart, many of these strategies protect confidentiality by restricting access to the data, either by limiting access to those data users who explicitly guarantee not to reveal respondent identities or attributes or by requiring that data users work in a restricted environment so they cannot remove information that might reveal identities or attributes. Restricting data access is a strategy that can be used with original data or with data that have been deidentified, buffered, or synthesized.

In addition to restricting access, institutional approaches require that researchers—students and faculty or staff at universities or other institutions—be educated in appropriate and ethical use of data. Many data stewards provide guidelines about how data should be used, what the risks of disclosure are, and why researchers should be attentive to disclosure risk and its limitation.[1]

User education at a more fundamental level—in the general training of active and future researchers—should be based on sound theoretical principles and empirical research. Such studies, however, are few: there are only a few examples of good materials or curricula for ensuring education in proper data use that minimizes the risk of confidentiality breaches. For instance, the disclosure limitation program project, "Human Subject Protection and Disclosure Risk Analysis," at the Inter-university Consortium for Political and Social Research (ICPSR) has resources available for teaching about its findings and the best practices it has developed (see http://www.icpsr.umich.edu/HSP [April 2006]). ICPSR is also working on a set of education and certification materials on handling restricted data for its own staff, which will probably evolve into formal training materials. The Carolina Population Center also has a set of practices for training students who work on its National Longitudinal Study of Adolescent Health (Add Health: see http://www.cpc.unc.edu/projects/addhealth [April 2006]) and other projects, and for teaching its demography trainees about ethics (see http://www.cpc.unc.edu/training/meth.html [April 2006]). However, few other training programs have equivalent practices.

Fundamental to most institutional approaches is the idea that the greater the risk of disclosure or harm, the more restricted access should be. For every tier of disclosure risk, there is an equivalent tier of access restriction. The tiers of risk are partly a function of the ability of the data distributor to make use of identity masking techniques to limit the risk of disclosure. On a low tier of risk are data with few identifiable variables, such as the public-use microdata sets from the U.S. Census Bureau and many small sample surveys. Because there is little or no geographic detail in these data, when they are anonymized there is very little risk of disclosure, although if a secondary user knows that an individual is a respondent in a survey (e.g., because it is a family member), identification is much easier. Dissemination of these data over the Web has not been problematic from the standpoint of confidentiality breaches. On the highest tier of risk are absolutely identifiable data, such as surveys of business establishments and data that include the exact locations of respondents' homes or workplaces.[2] The use of these data must be tightly restricted to preserve confidentiality. Methods and

---

[1]For example, see the Inter-university Consortium for Political and Social Research (ICPSR), 2005; also http://www.icpsr.umich.edu/access/deposit/index.html [accessed April 2006].

[2]Business establishments are generally considered to be among the most easily identifiable because data about them are frequently unique: in any given market, there are usually only a small number of business establishments engaged in any given area of activity, and each has unique characteristics such as relative size or specialization.

procedures for restricted data access are well described in a National Research Council report (2005a:28-34).

The number of tiers of access can vary from one study to another and from one data archive to another. A simple model might have four levels of access: full public access, limited licensing, strong licensing, and data enclaves.[3]

Full Public Access

Full access is provided through Web-based public-use files that are available to the general public or to a limited public (for example those who subscribe to a data service, such as ICPSR). Access is available to all users who accept a data use agreement through a Web-based form that requires them to avoid disclosure. This tier of access is typically reserved for data files with little risk of disclosure and harm, such as those that include very small subsamples of a larger sample, that represent a tiny fraction of the population in a geographic area, that contain little or no geographic information, or that do not include any sensitive information. We are unaware of any cases for which this form of public access is allowed to files that combine social data with highly specific locational data, such as addresses or exact latitude and longitude.

Public use, full-access datasets may include some locational data, such as neighborhood or census tract, if it is believed that such units are too broad to allow identification of particular individuals. However, when datasets are linked, it is often possible to identify individuals with high probability even when the linked data provide only neighborhood-level information. Because of this probability, the U.S. Census Bureau uses data swapping and other techniques in their full-access public-use data files (see http://factfinder.census.gov/jsp/saff/SAFFInfo.jsp?_pageId=su5_confidentiality).

Full public access is extremely popular with data users, for whom it provides a very high level of flexibility and opportunity. Their main complaint is that the datasets made available by this mechanism often include fewer cases and variables than they would like, so that certain types of analysis are impossible. Although data stewards appear generally satisfied

---

[3]For other models, see the practices of the Carolina Population Center at the University of North Carolina at Chapel Hill for use of data from the National Survey of Adolescent Health (http://www.cpc.unc.edu/projects/addhealth/data[accessed April 2006]) and the Nang Rong study of social and environmental change, among others. As part of ICPSR's Data Sharing for Demographic Research project (http://www.icpsr.umich.edu/dsdr [accessed April 2006]), researchers there have published a detailed review of contract terms used in restricted use agreements, with recommendations about how to construct such agreements. Those documents are available at http://www.icpsr.umich.edu/dsdr/rduc [accessed April 2006].

with this form of data distribution, they have in recent years begun to express concern about whether data can be shared this way without risk of disclosure, and so have increasingly restricted the number of data collections available in this format. For example, the National Center for Health Statistics (NCHS) linked the National Health Interview Survey to the National Death Index and made the first two releases of the linked file available publicly. The third release, which follows both respondents from the earlier survey years and adds new survey years, is no longer available publicly; it is available for restricted use in the NCHS Research Data Center.

Limited Licensing

Limited licensing provides a second tier of access for data that present some risk of disclosure or harm, but for which the risk is limited because there is little geographic precision—the geographic information has been systematically masked (Armstrong et al., 1999) or sensitive variables have been deleted or heavily masked. Limited licensing allows data to be distributed to responsible scientific data users (generally those affiliated with known academic institutions) under terms of a license that requires the data user and his or her employer to certify that the data will be used responsibly. Data stewards release data in this fashion when they believe that there is little risk of identification and that responsible professionals are able to understand the risk and prevent it in their research activities. For example, the Demographic and Health Surveys (DHS) (see http://www.measuredhs. com/[April 2006]) distributes its large representative survey data collection under a limited licensing model. It makes geocoded data available under a more restricted type of limited licensing arrangement.

The DHS collects the geographic coordinates of its survey cluster, or enumerator areas, but the boundaries or areas of those regions are not made available. These geocodes can be attached to individual or household records in the survey data, for which identifying information has been removed. When particularly sensitive information has been collected in the survey (e.g., HIV testing), the current policy is to introduce error into the data, destroy the original data, and release only the data that have been transformed.

Data users consider it a burden to obtain limited licensing agreements, but both data stewards and users generally perceive them as successful because they combine an obligation for education and certification with relatively flexible access for datasets that present little risk of disclosure or harm. Nevertheless, the limitations on the utility of data that may be altered (see Armstrong et al., 1999) for release in this manner are still largely unknown, in part because careful tests with the original data cannot be conducted after the data have been transformed.

Strong Licensing

Strong licensing is a third tier of data access used for data that present a substantial risk of disclosure and for which the data steward decides that this risk cannot be protected within the framework of responsible research practice. Datasets are typically placed at this tier if they present a substantial risk of disclosure but are not fully identified or if they include attribute data that are highly sensitive if disclosed, such as responses about sexual practices, drug use, or criminal activity. Most often, these data are shared through a license that requires special handling: for example, they may be kept on a single computer not connected to a network, with specific technical requirements. Virtually all strong licenses require that the data user obtain institutional review board (IRB) approval at his or her home institution. Many of these strong licenses also include physical monitoring, such as unannounced visits from the data steward's staff to make sure that conditions are followed. These licenses may also require very strong institutional assurances from the researcher's employer, or may provide for sanctions if not followed. For example, the license to use data from the Health and Retirement Survey of the National Institutes of Health (NIH) includes language that says the data user may be prevented from obtaining NIH grants in the future if he or she does not adhere to the restrictions. Some data stewards also require the payment of a fee, usually in the range of $500 to $1,000, to support the expenses associated with document preparation and review and the cost of site visits.

Although some researchers and universities are wary of these agreements, in recent years they have been seen as successful by most data users. Data distributors, however, continue to be fearful that their rules about data access are not being followed sufficiently closely or that sensitive data are under inadequate control.

Data Enclaves

For data that present the greatest risk of disclosure or harm, or those that are collected under tight legal restrictions—such as geospatial data that are absolutely identifiable—access is usually limited to use within a research enclave. For example, this will be the case when the fully geocoded Nang Rong data are made available at the data enclave at ICPSR. The most visible example of this practice in the United States today is the network of nine Research Data Centers (RDCs) created by the Bureau of the Census—Washington, DC; Durham, NC; New York City and Ithaca, NY; Boston, MA; Ann Arbor, MI; Chicago; and Los Angeles and Berkeley, CA.[4] The

---

[4]See http://webserver01.ces.census.gov/index.php/ces/1.00/researchlocations [accessed April 2006].

Bureau makes its most restricted data, including the full count of the Census of Population and the Census of Business Enterprises, available only in these centers.

The principle behind data enclaves is that researchers are not able to leave the premises with any information that might identify an individual. In practice, a trained professional reviews all the materials that each researcher prints. For data analyses, researchers are typically allowed to remove only coefficients from regression-type analyses and tabulations that have a large cell size (because small cell sizes may lead to identification). Although many data stewards limit users to working within a single, supervised room described as a data center or enclave, alternatives also exist. For example, in addition to its data enclaves NCHS also maintains a system that allows data users to submit data analytic programs from a remote location, have them run against the data in the enclave, and then receive the results by e-mail. This procedure is sometimes performed with an automated disclosure review and sometimes with a manual, expert review.

There are considerable barriers of inconvenience and cost to use of the data centers, which means that they are not used as much as they might or should be. Most centers only hold data from a single data provider (for example, the census, NCHS data, or ADD Health), and the division of work leads to inefficiencies that might be overcome if a single center held data from more than one data provider. For the use of its data, the Census Bureau centers require a lengthy approval process that can take a full year from the time a researcher is ready to begin work, as well as a "benefit statement" on the part of the researcher that demonstrates the work undertaken in the RDC will not only contribute to science, but will also deliver a benefit to the Census Bureau—something required by the Bureau's statutory authority. Although other data centers and enclaves do not require such lengthy approval processes, many require a substantial financial payment from the researcher (often calculated as a per day or per month cost of research center use), in addition to travel and lodging costs. Personal scheduling to enable a researcher to travel to a remote site competes with teaching, institutional service, and personal obligations and can be a serious barrier to use of data in enclaves. The challenge of scheduling becomes even more severe in the context of the large, interdisciplinary teams often involved in the analysis of spatial social science data and the need to use specialized technology and software. In addition to the cost passed on to users, the data stewards who maintain data enclaves bear considerable cost and space requirements.

In sum, data enclaves are effective but inefficient and inequitable. Social science research is faced with the prospect of full and equal access to data when risk is low, but highly differential and unequal access when risks are high. Considerable improvements in data access regimes will be required so that price will not be the mediating factor that determines who has access to linked social science and geospatial data.

TECHNICAL APPROACHES

Data stewards and statistical researchers have developed a variety of techniques for limiting disclosure risks (for a summary of many of them, see National Research Council, 2005a). This section briefly reviews some of these methods and discusses their strengths and weaknesses in the context of spatial data. Generally, we classify the solutions as data limitation (releasing only some of the data), data alteration (releasing perturbed versions of the data), and data simulation (releasing data that were not collected from respondents but that are intended to perform as the original data when analyzed). The approaches described here are designed to preserve as much spatial information as possible because that information is necessary for important research questions. In this way, they represent advances over older approaches to creating public-use social science data, in which the near-universal strategy was to delete all precise spatial information from the data, usually through aggregation to large areas.

Data Limitation

Data limitation involves manipulations that restrict the number of variables, the number of values for responses, or the number of cases that are made available to researchers. The purpose of data limitation is to reduce the number of unique values in a dataset (reducing the risk of identification) or to reduce the certainty of identification of a specific respondent by a secondary user. A very simple approach sometimes taken with public-use data is to release only a small fraction of the data originally collected, effectively deleting half or more of all cases. This approach makes it difficult, even impossible, for a secondary user who knows that an individual is in the sample to be sure that she or he has identified the right person: the target individual may have been among those deleted from the public dataset.

For tabular data, as well as some microdata, one data limitation approach is cell suppression. The data steward essentially blanks out cells with small counts in tabular data or blanks out the values of identifiers or sensitive attributes in microdata. The definition of "small counts" is selected by the data steward. Frequently, cells in tables are not released unless they have at least three members. When marginal totals are preserved, as is often planned in tabular data, other values besides those at risk may need to be suppressed; otherwise, the data analyst can subtract the sum of the available values from the total to obtain the value of the suppressed data.

Complementary cells are selected to optimize (at least approximately) various mathematical criteria. (For discussions of cell suppression, see Cox, 1980, 1995; Willenborg and de Waal, 1996, 2001.)

Cell suppression has drawbacks. It creates missing data, which complicates analyses because the suppressed cells are chosen for their values and are not randomly distributed throughout the dataset. When there are many records at risk, as is likely to be the case for spatial data with identifiers, data disseminators may need to suppress so many values to achieve satisfactory levels of protection that the released data have limited analytical utility. Cell suppression is not necessarily helpful for preserving confidentiality in survey data that include precise geospatial locations. It is possible, even if some or many cells are suppressed, for confidentiality to be breached if locational data remain. Cell suppression also does not guarantee protection in tabular data: it may be possible to determine accurate bounds for values of the suppressed cells using statistical techniques (Cox, 2004; Fienberg and Slavkovic, 2004, 2005). An alternative to cell suppression in tabular data is controlled tabular adjustment, which adds noise to cell counts in ways that preserve certain analyses (Cox et al., 2004).

Data can also be limited by aggregation. For tabular data, aggregation corresponds to collapsing levels of categorical variables to increase the cell size for each level. For microdata, aggregation corresponds to coarsening variables; for example, releasing ages in 5-year intervals or locations at the state level in the United States. Aggregation reduces disclosure risks by turning unique records into replicated records. It preserves analyses at the level of aggregation but creates ecological inference problems for lower levels of aggregation.

For spatial data, stewards can aggregate spatial identifiers or attribute values or both, but the aggregation of spatial identifiers is especially important. Aggregating spatial attributes puts more than one respondent into a single spatial location, which may be a point (latitude-longitude), a line (e.g., along a highway), or an area of various shapes (e.g., a census tract or other geographic division or a geometrically defined area, such as a circle). This aggregation has the effect of eliminating unique cases within the dataset or eliminating the possibility that a location in the data refers to only a single individual in some other data source, such as a map or list of addresses. In essence, this approach coarsens the geographic data.

Some disclosure limitation policies prohibit the release of information at any level of aggregation smaller than a county. Use of a fixed level of geography, however, introduces variability in the degree of masking provided. Many rural counties in the United States contain very small total populations, on the order of 1 thousand, while urban counties may contain more than 1 million people. The same problem arises with geographic areas defined by spatial coverage: 1 urban square kilometer holds many more people than

1 rural square kilometer. The more social identifiers, such as gender, race, or age, are provided for an area, the greater the risk of disclosure.

The use of aggregation to guard against accidental release of confidential information introduces side effects into analyses. When point data are aggregated to areas that are sufficiently large to maintain confidentiality, the ability of researchers to analyze data for spatial patterns is attenuated. Clusters of disease that may be visually evident or statistically significant at the individual level, for example, will often become undetectable at the county level of aggregation. Other effects arise as a consequence of the well-known relationship between variance and aggregation: variance tends to decrease as the size of aggregated units increase (see Robinson, 1950; Clark and Avery, 1976). The suppression of variance with increasing levels of aggregation introduces uncertainty (sometimes called the ecological inference problem) into the process of making inferences based on statistical analyses and is a component of the more general modifiable areal unit problem in spatial data analysis (see Openshaw and Taylor, 1979).

For tabular data, another data limitation alternative is to release a selection of subtables or collapsed tables of marginal totals for some properties to ensure that the cells for the full joint table are large (Fienberg and Slavkovic, 2004, 2005). This approach preserves the possibility of analysis when counts from the released subtables are sufficient for the analysis. For spatial data, this approach could be used with aggregated spatial identifiers, perhaps enabling smaller amounts of aggregation. This approach is computationally expensive, especially for high-dimensional tables, and requires additional research before a more complete assessment can be made of its effectiveness.

Data Alteration

Spatial attributes are useful in linked social-spatial data because they precisely record where an aspect of a respondent's life takes place. Sometimes these spatial data are collected at the moment that the original social survey data are collected. In the Nang Rong (see Box 1-1) and other similar studies, researchers use a portable global positioning system (GPS) device to record the latitude and longitude of the location of the interview or of multiple locations (farm fields, daily itineraries) during the interview process. It is also possible for researchers to follow the daily itineraries of study participants by use of GPS devices or RFID (radio frequency identification) tags.

In the United States and other developed countries, however, locations are frequently collected not as latitude and longitude from a GPS device, but by asking an individual to supply a street address. Street addresses require some transformation (e.g., to latitude and longitude) to be made specific and comparable. This transformation, called geocoding, consists of the processes through which physical locations are added to records. There are several types of geocoding that vary in their level of specificity; each approach uses different materials to support the assignment of coordinates to records (see Box 3-1).

Areal geocoding can reduce the likelihood of identification, but most other forms of geocoding have the potential to maintain or increase the risk of disclosure because they provide the data user with one or more precise locations (identifiers) for a survey respondent. The improvements in accuracy associated with new data sources and new technologies, such as parcel geocoding, only heighten the risk. As a consequence, a new set of techniques has been devised to distort locations, and hence to inhibit disclosure. Two of the general methods available are swapping and masking.

Swapping It is sometimes possible to limit disclosure risk by swapping data. For example, a data steward can swap the attributes of a person in one area for those of a person in another area, especially if some of those attributes are the same (such as two 50-year-old white males with different responses on other questions), in order to reduce a secondary user's confidence in correctly identifying an individual. Swapping can be done on spatial identifiers or nonspatial attributes, and it can be done within or across defined geographic locations. Swapping small fractions of data generally attenuates associations between the swapped and unswapped variables, and swapping large fractions of data can completely destroy those associations. Swapping data will make spatial analyses meaningless unless the spatial relationships have been carried into the swapped data. It is generally difficult for analysts of swapped data to know how much the swapping affects the quality of analyses.

When data stewards swap cases from different locations but leave (genuine) exact spatial identifiers on the file, the identity of participants may be disclosed, even if attributes cannot be meaningfully linked to the participant. For example, if the data reveal that a respondent lived at a particular address, even if that person's data are swapped with someone else's data, a secondary user would still know that a person living at that address was included in the study. Swapping spatial identifiers thus is better suited for limiting disclosures of respondents' attributes than their identities. Swapping may not reduce—and probably increases—the risk of mistaken attribute disclosures from incorrect identifications.

Swapping may be more successful at protecting participants' identities when locations are aggregated. However, swapping may not provide much additional protection beyond the aggregation of locations, and it may decrease data quality relative to analyzing the unswapped aggregated data.

BOX 3-1
Geocoding Methods

Areal Geocoding Areal geocoding assigns observations to geographic areas. If all a researcher needs is to assign a respondent to a political jurisdiction, census unit, or administrative or other areas in order to match attributes of those larger areas to the individual and perform hierarchical analyses, areal geocoding resolution is a valuable tool. Areal geocoding can be implemented when the database has either addresses or latitude and longitude data, either through the use of a list of addresses that are contained in an area or through the use of an algorithm that determines whether a point is contained within a particular polygon in space. In the latter case, a digital file of polygon geometry is needed to support the areal geocoding process.

Interpolated Geocoding Interpolated geocoding estimates the precise location of an address along a street segment, typically defined between street intersections, on a proportional basis. This approach relies on the use of a geographic base file (GBF) that contains street centerline descriptions and address ranges for each side of each street segment in the coverage area. An example is the U.S. Census Bureau's TIGER (topologically integrated geographic encoding and referencing) files. For any specific address, an algorithm assigns coordinates to records by finding the street segment (typically, one side of a block along a street) that contains the address and interpolating. Thus, the address 1225 Maple Street would be placed one-quarter of the way along the block that contains the odd-numbered addresses 1201-1299 and assigned the latitude and longitude appropriate to that precise point.

Interpolated geocoding can produce digital artifacts, such as addresses placed in the middle of a curving street, or errors, such as can occur if, for example, 1225 is the last house on the 1201 block of Maple Street. Some of these problems can

Masking Masking involves perturbations or transformations of some data. Observations, in some cases, may be represented as points, but have their locations altered in such a way to minimize accurate recovery of personal-level information. Among the easiest masking approaches to implement involves the addition of a stochastic component to each observation, which can be visualized as moving the point by a fixed or random amount so that the information about a respondent is associated not with that person's true location but with another location (see Chakraborty and Armstrong, 2001). That is, one can replace an accurately located point with another point derived from a uniform distribution of radius r centered on that location. The radius parameter may be constant or allowed to vary as a function of density or some other factor important to a particular application. If density is used, r will be large in low-density areas (rural) and would be adjusted downward in areas with higher densities.

be minimized with software (e.g., by setting houses back from streets). The extent to which such data transformations change the results of data analyses from what they would have been with untransformed data has not been carefully studied. This approach may reduce disclosure risks.

Parcel Geocoding Parcel geocoding makes use of new cadastral information systems that have been implemented in many communities. When this approach is used, coordinates are often transferred from registered digital orthophotographs (images that have been processed to remove distortion that arises as a consequence of sensor geometry and variability in local elevation, for example). These coordinates typically represent such features as street curbs and centerlines, sidewalks, and most importantly for geocoding, the locations of parcel and building footprint polygons and either parcel centroids or building footprint centroids. Thus, a one-to-one correspondence between each address and an accurate coordinate (representing the building or parcel centroid) can be established during geocoding. This approach typically yields more accurate positional information than interpolated geocoding methods.

GNSS-based Geocoding The low cost and widespread availability of devices used to measure location based on signals provided by Global Navigation Satellite Systems (GNSS), such as the Global Positioning System deployed by the U.S. Department of Defense, GLONASS (Russia), and Galileo (European Union), has encouraged some practitioners to record coordinate locations for residence locations through field observations. As in the parcel approach, a one-to-one correspondence can be established between each residence and an associated coordinate. Though this process is somewhat labor intensive, the results are typically accurate since trained field workers can make policy-driven judgments about how to record particular kinds of information.

Though masking can be performed easily, it has a negative side effect: the displaced points can be assigned to locations that contain real observations, thus creating the possibility of false identification and harm to individuals who may not even be respondents in the research. Moreover, research on spatial data transformation that involve moving the location of data points (Armstrong et al., 1999; Rushton et al., 2006) shows that these transformations may have a significant deleterious effect on the analysis of data. Not only is there still risk of false identification, but sometimes the points are placed in locations where they cannot be—residences in lakes that do not permit houseboats, for example. Moreover, no single transformation process provides data that are valuable for every possible form of analysis. These limitations have major consequences both for successful analysis and for reduction of the disclosure risk.

Adding noise generally inflates uncertainties in data analyses. For some attributes being estimated, the effect is to increase the width of confidence intervals. Adding noise can also attenuate associations: in a simple linear regression model, for example, the estimated regression coefficients get closer to zero when the predictors have extra noise. There are techniques for accounting for the extra noise, called measurement error models (e.g., Fuller, 1993), but they are not easy to use except in such standard analyses as regressions. Some research by computer scientists and cryptographers under the rubric of "privacy-preserving data mining" (e.g., Agrawal and Srikant, 2000; Chawla et al., 2005) also follows the strategy of adding specially constructed random noise to the data, either to individual values or to the results of the computations desired by the analyst. Privacy-preserving data mining approaches have been developed for regression analysis, for clustering algorithms, for discrimination, and for association rules. Like other approaches that add noise, these approaches generally sacrifice data quality for protection against disclosure. The nature of that tradeoff has not been thoroughly evaluated for social and spatial data.

Secure Access

An emerging set of techniques aims to provide users with the results of computations on data without allowing them to see individual data values. Some of these are based on variants of secure summation (Benaloh, 1987), which allows different data stewards to compute the exact values of sums without sharing their values. One variant, used at the National Center for Educational Statistics, provides public data on a diskette or CD-ROM that is encoded to allow users to construct special tabulations while preventing them from seeing the individual-level data or for calculating totals when there are fewer than 30 respondents in a cell. Secure summation variants entail no sacrifice in data quality for analyses based on sums. They provide excellent confidentiality protection, as long as the database stewards follow specified protocols. This approach is computationally intensive and challenging to set up (for a review of these methods, see Karr et al., 2005).

Another approach involves remote access model servers, to which users submit requests for analyses and, in return, receive only the results of statistical analyses, such as estimated model parameters and standard errors. Confidentiality can be protected because the remote server never allows users to see the actual data (see Boulos et al., 2006). Remote access servers do not protect perfectly, however, as the user may be able to learn identities or sensitive attributes through judicious queries of the system (for examples, see Gomatam et al., 2005). Computer scientists also have developed methods for secure record linkage, which enable two or more data stewards to determine which records in their databases have the same values of unique identifiers without revealing the values of identifiers for the other records in their databases (Churches and Christen, 2004; O'Keefe et al., 2004).

Secure access approaches have not generally been used by stewards of social science data, and the risks and benefits for spatial-social data dissemination and sharing are largely unevaluated. However, the concept underpinning these techniques—to allow users to perform computations with the data without actually seeing the data—may point to solutions for sharing social and spatial data.

Data Simulation

Data providers may also release synthetic (i.e., simulated) data that have similar characteristics as the genuine data as a way to preserve both confidentiality and the possibility of meaningful data analysis, an approach first proposed by Rubin (1993) in the statistical literature. The basic idea is to fit probability models to the original data, then simulate and release new data that fit the same models. Because the data are simulated, the released records do not correspond to individuals from the original file and cannot be directly linked to records in other datasets. These features greatly reduce identity and attribute disclosure risks. However, synthetic data are subject to inferential disclosure risk when the models used to generate data are too accurate. For example, when data are simulated from a regression model with a very small mean square error, analysts can use the model to estimate outcomes precisely and can infer the identities of respondents with high accuracy.

When the probability models closely approximate the true joint probability distributions of the actual data, the synthetic data should have similar characteristics, on average. The "on average" caveat is important: parameter estimates from any one synthetic dataset are unlikely to equal exactly those from the actual data. The synthetic parameter estimates are subject to variation from sampling the collected data and from simulating new values. It is not possible to estimate all sources of variation from only one synthetic dataset, because an analyst cannot measure the amount of variability from the synthesis. Rubin's (1993) suggestion is to simulate and release multiple, independent synthetic data sets from the same original data. An analyst can then estimate parameters and their variances in each of the synthetic datasets and combine the results with simple formulas (see description by Raghunathan et al., 2003).

Synthetic datasets can have many positive data utility features (see Rubin, 1993; Raghunathan et al., 2003; Reiter, 2002, 2004, 2005b). When the data generation models are accurate, valid inferences can be obtained from multiple synthetic datasets by combining standard likelihood-based or survey-weighted estimates. An analyst need not learn new statistical methods or software programs to unwind the effects of the disclosure limitation method. Synthetic datasets can be generated as simple random samples, so that analysts can ignore the original complex sampling design for inferences. The data generation models can adjust for nonsampling errors and can borrow strength from other data sources, thereby making high-quality inferences possible. Finally, because all units are simulated, geographic identifiers can be included in synthetic datasets.

Synthetic data reflect only those relationships included in the models used to generate them. When the models fail to reflect certain relationships, analysts' inferences also do not reflect those relationships. For example, if the data generation model for an attribute does not take into account relationships between location and that attribute, the synthetic data will contain zero association between the spatial data and that attribute. Similarly, incorrect distributional assumptions built into the models are passed on to the users' analyses. For example, if the data generation model for an attribute is a normal distribution when the actual distribution is skewed, the synthetic data will fail to reflect the shape of the actual distribution. If a model does fail to include such relationships, it is a potentially serious limitation to releasing fully synthetic data. Practically, it means that some analyses cannot be performed accurately and that data disseminators need to release information that helps analysts decide whether or not the synthetic data are reliable for their analyses.

To reduce dependency on data generation models, Little (1993) suggests a variant of the fully synthetic data approach called partially synthetic data. Imagine a data set with three kinds of information: information that, when combined, is a potential indirect identifier of the respondent (age, sex, race, occupation, and spatial location); information that is potentially highly sensitive (responses about antisocial or criminal behavior, for example); and a residual body of information that is less sensitive and less likely to lead to identification (responses about personal values or nonsensitive behaviors). Partially synthetic data might synthesize the first two categories of data, while retaining the actual data of the third category. For example, the U.S. Federal Reserve Board protects data in the U.S. Survey of Consumer Finances by replacing monetary values at high disclosure risk with multiple imputations, releasing a mixture of these imputed values and the unreplaced, actual values (Kennickell, 1997). The U.S. Bureau of the Census protects data in longitudinal linked data sets by replacing all values of some sensitive variables with multiple imputations and leaving other variables at their actual values (Abowd and Woodcock, 2001). Partially synthetic approaches promise to maintain the primary benefits of fully synthetic data—protecting confidentiality while allowing users to make inferences without learning complicated statistical methods or software—with decreased sensitivity to the specification of the data generation models (Reiter, 2003).

The protection afforded by partially synthetic data depends on the nature of the synthesis. Replacing key identifiers with imputations obscures the original values of those identifiers, which reduces the chance of identifications. Replacing values of sensitive variables obscures the exact values of those variables, which can prevent attribute disclosures. Partially synthetic datasets present greater disclosure risks than fully synthetic ones: the originally sampled units remain in the released files, albeit with some values changed, leaving values that analysts can use for record linkages.

Currently, for either fully or partially synthetic data, there are no semi-automatic data synthesizers. Data generation models are tailored to individual variables, using sequential regression modeling strategies (Raghunathan et al., 2001) and modifications of bootstrapping, among others. Substantial modeling expertise is required to develop valid synthesizers, as well as to evaluate the disclosure risks and data utility of the resulting datasets. Modeling poses an operational challenge to generating synthetic datasets. A few evaluations of the disclosure risk and data utility issues have been done with social surveys, but none with linked spatial-social data.

For spatially identifiable data, a fully synthetic approach simulates all spatial identifiers and all attributes. Such an approach can be achieved either by first generating new values of spatial identifiers, (for example, sampling addresses randomly from the population list, and then simulating attribute values tied to those new values of identifiers) or by first generating new attribute values and then simulating new spatial identifiers tied to those new attribute values. In generating new identifiers, however, care should be taken to avoid implausible or impossible results (e.g., private property on public lands, residences in uninhabitable areas). Either way, the synthesis requires models relating the geographic identifiers to the attributes. Contextual variables can provide information for modeling. The implications of these methods for data utility, and particularly for the validity of inferences drawn from linked social-spatial data synthesized by different methods, have not yet been studied empirically.

Fully synthetic records cannot be directly linked to records in other datasets, which reduces data utility when linkage is desired. One possibility for linkage is to make linkages informed by statistical analyses that attempt to match synthetic records in one dataset with appropriate nonsynthesized records in another dataset. Research has not been conducted to determine how well such matching preserves data utility.

Partially synthetic approaches can be used to simulate spatial identifiers or attributes. Simulating only the identifiers reduces disclosure risks without distorting relationships among the attribute variables. Its effect on the relationships between spatial and nonspatial variables depends on the quality of the synthesis model. At present, not much is known about the utility of this approach.

Linking datasets on synthetic identifiers or on attributes creates matching errors, and relationships between spatial identifiers and the linked variables may be attenuated. Analyses involving the synthetic identifiers reflect the assumptions in the model used to generate new identifier values on the basis of attribute values. This approach introduces error into matches obtained by linking the partially synthetic records to records in other datasets. Alternatively, simulating selected attributes reduces attribute risks without disturbing the identifiers: this enables linking, but it does not prevent identity disclosures. Relationships between the synthetic attributes and the linked attributes are attenuated—although to an as yet unknown degree—when the synthesizing models are not conditional on the linked attributes. This limitation also holds true when linking to fully synthetic data.

The release of partially synthetic data can be combined with other disclosure limitation methods. For example, the Census Bureau has an application, *On the Map* (http://lehdmap.dsd.census.gov/), that combines synthetic data and the addition of noise. Details of the procedure, which coarsens some workplace characteristics and generates synthetic travel origins conditional on travel destinations and workplace characteristics, have not yet been published.

4

The Tradeoff:
Confidentiality Versus Access

The previous three chapters describe the challenge of preserving confidentiality while facilitating research in an era of increasingly detailed and available data about research participants and their geographic locations. This chapter presents the committee's conclusions about what can—and cannot—be done to achieve two goals: ensure that both explicit and implied pledges of confidentiality are kept when social data are made spatially explicit and provide access to important research data for analysts working on significant basic and policy research questions. Following our conclusions, we offer recommendations for data stewards, researchers, and research funders.

CONCLUSIONS

Tradeoffs of Benefits and Risks

Recognition of the Benefits and Risks Making social data spatially explicit creates benefits and risks that must be considered in ethical guidelines and research policy. Spatially precise and accurate data about individuals, groups, or organizations, added to data records through processes of geocoding, make it possible for researchers to examine questions they could not otherwise explore and gain better understanding of human actors in their physical and environmental contexts, and they create benefits for society in terms of the knowledge that can flow from that research.

CONCLUSION 1: Recent advances in the availability of social and spatial data and the development of geographic information systems (GIS) and related techniques to manage and analyze those data give researchers important new ways to study important social, environmental, economic, and health policy issues and are worth further development.

Sharing of linked social-spatial data among researchers is imperative to get the most from the time, effort, and money that goes into obtaining the data. However, to the extent that data are spatially precise and accurate, the risk increases that the people or organizations that are the subject of the data can be identified. Promises of confidentiality that are normally provided for research participants and that can be kept when data are not linked could be jeopardized as a result of the data linkage, increasing the risk of disclosure and possibly also of harm, particularly when linked data are made available to secondary data users who may, for example, combine the linked data with other spatially explicit information about respondents that enables new kinds of analysis and, potentially, new kinds of harm. These risks affect not only research participants, but also the scientific enterprise that depends on participants' confidence in promises of confidentiality.

Researcher's Obligations Researchers who collect or undertake secondary analysis of linked social-spatial data and organizations that support research or provide access to such data have an ethical obligation to maximize the benefits of the research and minimize the risk of breaches of confidentiality to research participants. This obligation exists even if legal obligations are not clearly defined. Those who collect, analyze, or provide access to such data need to articulate strong data protection plans, stipulate conditions of access, and safeguard against possible breaches of confidentiality through all phases of the research—from data collection through dissemination. Protecting against any breach of confidentiality is a priority for researchers, in light of the need to honor confidentiality agreements between research participants and researchers, and to support public confidence in the integrity of the research.

The Tradeoff of Confidentiality and Access Restricting data access affords the highest protection to the confidentiality of linked social-spatial data that include exact locations. However, the costs to science are high. If confidentiality has been promised, common public-use forms of data distribution create unacceptable risks to confidentiality. Consequently, only more restrictive forms of data management and dissemination are appropriate, including extensive data reduction, strong licenses, and data center (enclave) access. When the precise data are available only in data enclaves, many researchers simply do not use the datasets, so research that could be done is not undertaken. Improved methods for providing remote access to enclave data require research and development efforts.

CONCLUSION 2: The increasing use of linked social-spatial data has created significant uncertainties about the ability to protect the confidentiality promised to research participants. Knowledge is as yet inadequate concerning the conditions under which and the extent to which the availability of spatially explicit data about participants increases the risk of confidentiality breaches.

The risks created by the availability and publication of such information increases the better-known risks associated with other publication-related breaches of confidentiality, such as the publication of the names or locations of primary sampling units or of specific tabular cell sizes. For example, cartographic materials are often used in publications to illustrate points or findings that do not lend themselves as easily to tabular or text explication: what is not yet understood are the conditions under which they also increase the ability to identify a research participant.

Technical Strategies for Reducing Risk

Cell Suppression, Data Swapping, and Aggregation Cell suppression and data swapping techniques can protect confidentiality, but they seriously degrade the value of data for analyses in which spatial information is essential. Aggregation can provide adequate protection and preserves analysis at a level of aggregation, but it renders data useless when exact locations are required. Hence, aggregation has merit for data that have low levels of risk and are slated for public-use dissemination, but not for data that will be used for analyses that require exact spatial information.

When analyses require exact locations, essentially all observations are the equivalent of small cells in a statistical table: cell suppression would therefore be tantamount to destroying the spatial component of the data. Suppressing nonspatial attributes leaves so much missing information that the data are difficult to analyze. Swapping exact locations may not prevent identifications and can create serious distortions in analysis when a location or a topological relationship is a critical variable. Swapping nonspatial attributes to limit attribute disclosure risk may need to be done at so high a rate that the associations in the data are badly attenuated. Suppression or swapping can be used to preserve confidentiality when analyses require inexact levels of geography, but aggregation is a superior approach in these cases because it preserves analyses at those levels. Aggregation makes it impossible to perform many types of analyses, and when it is used it can lead to ecological inference problems.

Data Alteration Data alteration methods, such as geographic masking or adding noise to sensitive nonspatial attributes, may improve confidentiality protection but at the expense of data quality. Altering data to mask precise spatial locations impedes the ability of researchers to calculate accurate spatial relationships, such as distances, directions, and inclusion of locations within an enumeration unit (e.g., a census tract). There is a tradeoff between the magnitude of any masking displacement and the corresponding utility of an observation for a particular use. Decisions about this tradeoff affect the risk of a breach of confidentiality. A mask may also be applied to nonspatial attributes associated with known locations: this might be done when knowledge about the magnitude of an attribute, along with knowledge about a generating process (such as a deterministic model of toxic emissions), could enable the recovery of a location that could then be linked to other information.

Synthetic Data Synthetic data approaches may have the potential to provide access to data with exact spatial identifiers while preserving confidentiality. There is insufficient evidence at present to determine how well this approach preserves the social-spatial relationships of interest to researchers. In addition, with current technologies, it is very difficult for data stewards to create analytically valid synthetic datasets. The goal of synthetic data approaches is to protect confidentiality while preserving certain relationships in the data. This approach depends on data simulation models that capture the relationships among the spatial and nonspatial variables. The effectiveness of such models has not been fully demonstrated across a wide range of analyses and datasets. For example, it is not known how well these models can preserve distance and topological relationships. It is also not known whether and how the various synthetic data approaches can be applied when linking datasets.

Secure Access Techniques for providing secure access to linked data, such as sharing sums but not individual values or conducting data analyses on request and returning the results but not the data may have the potential to provide results from spatial analyses without revealing data values. These approaches are not yet extensively used by stewards of spatial data, and their feasibility for social and spatial data is unproven. They are computationally intensive and require expertise that is not available to many data stewards. The value of some of these methods is limited by restrictions on the total number of queries that can be performed before queries could be combined to identify elements in the original data.

CONCLUSION 3: Recent research on technical approaches for reducing the risk of identification and breach of confidentiality has demonstrated promise for future success. At this time, however, no known technical strategy or combination of technical strategies for managing linked social-spatial data adequately resolves conflicts among the objectives of data linkage, open access, data quality, and confidentiality protection across datasets and data uses.

In our judgment, it will remain difficult to reconcile these conflicting objectives by technical strategies alone, though efforts to identify effective methods and procedures should continue. It is likely that different methods and procedures will be optimal for different applications and that the best approaches will evolve with the data and with techniques for protecting confidentiality and for identifying respondents.

Institutional Approaches

CONCLUSION 4: Because technical strategies will be not be sufficient in the foreseeable future for resolving the conflicting demands for data access, data quality, and confidentiality, institutional approaches will be required to balance those demands.

Institutional approaches involve establishing tiers of risk and access and producing data-sharing solutions that match levels of access to the risks and benefits of the planned research. Institutional approaches must address issues of shared responsibility for the production, control, and use of data among primary data producers, secondary producers who link additional information, data users of all kinds, research sponsors, IRBs, government agencies, and data stewards. It is essential that the power to decide about data access and use be allocated appropriately among these responsible actors and that those with the greatest power to decide are highly informed about the issues and about the benefits and risks of the data access policies they may be asked to approve. It is also essential that users of the data bear the burden of confidentiality protection for the data they use.

RECOMMENDATIONS

We generally endorse the recommendations of two reports, *Protecting Participants and Facilitating Social and Behavioral Sciences Research* (National Research Council, 2003) and *Expanding Access to Research Data: Reconciling Risks and Opportunities* (National Research Council, 2005a) regarding general issues of confidentiality and data access. It is important to note that the recommendations in those reports address only data collected and held by federal agencies, and they do not deal with the special issues that arise when social and spatial data are linked. This report extends those recommendations to include the large body of data that are collected by individual researchers and academic and research organizations and held at universities and other public research entities. It also addresses the need for research sponsors, research organizations such as universities, and researchers to pay special attention to data that record exact locations.

In particular, we support several key recommendations of these reports:

• Access to data should be provided "through a variety of modes, including various modes of restricted access to confidential data and unrestricted access to public-use data altered in a variety of ways to maintain confidentiality" (National Research Council, 2005a:68).

• Organizations that sponsor data collection should "conduct or sponsor research on techniques for providing useful, innovative public-use data that minimize the risk of disclosure" (National Research Council, 2005a:72) and continue efforts to "develop and implement state-of-the-art disclosure protection practices and methods (National Research Council, 2003:4).

• Organizations that sponsor data collection "should conduct or sponsor research on cost-effective means of providing secure access to confidential data by means of a remote access mechanism, consistent with their confidentiality assurance protocols" (National Research Council, 2005a:78).

• Data stewardship organizations that use licensing agreements should "expand the files for which a license may be obtained [and] work with data users to develop flexible, consistent standards for licensing agreements and implementation procedures for access to confidential data" (National Research Council, 2005a:79).

• Professional associations should develop strong codes of ethical conduct and should provide training in ethical issues for "all those involved in the design, collection, distribution, and use of data collected under pledges of confidentiality" (National Research Council, 2005a:84).

Some of these recommendations will not be straightforward to implement for datasets that link social and spatially explicit data. We therefore elaborate on those recommendations for the special issues and tradeoffs raised by linking social and spatial data.

Technical and Institutional Research

RECOMMENDATION 1: Federal agencies and other organizations that sponsor the collection and analysis of linked social-spatial data—

or that support data that could provide added benefits with such link-age—should sponsor research into techniques and procedures for dis-seminating such data while protecting confidentiality and maintain-ing the usefulness of the data for social and spatial analysis. This research should include studies to adapt existing techniques from other fields, to understand how the publication of linked social-spatial data might increase disclosure risk, and to explore institutional mechanisms for disseminating linked data while protecting confidentiality and main-taining the usefulness of the data.

This research should include three elements. First, it should include studies that focus on both adapting existing techniques and developing new approaches in social science, computer science, geographical science, and statistical science that have the potential to deal effectively with the prob-lems of linked social-spatial data. The research should include assessments of the disclosure risk, data quality, and implementation feasibility associ-ated with the techniques, as well as seeking to identify ways for data stew-ards to make these assessments for their data.

This line of research should include work on techniques that enable data analysts to understand what analyses can be reliably done with shared data. It should also include research on analytical methods that correct or at least account for the effects of data alteration. Finally, the research should be done through collaborations among data stewards, data users, and researchers in the appropriate sciences. Among the most promising techniques are spatial aggregation, geographic masking, fully and partially synthetic data and remote access model servers and other emerging meth-ods of secure access and secure record linkage.

Second, the research should include work to understand how the pub-lication of spatially explicit material using linked social-spatial data might increase disclosure risk and thus to increase sensitivity to this issue. The research would include assessments of disclosure risk associated with carto-graphic displays. It should involve researchers from the social, spatial, and statistical sciences and would aim to better understand how the public presentation of cartographic and other spatially explicit information could affect the risk of confidentiality breaches. The education should involve researchers, data stewards, reviewers and journal editors.

Third, the research should work on institutional mechanisms for dis-seminating linked social-spatial data while protecting confidentiality and maintaining the usefulness of the data for social and spatial analysis. This research should include studies of modifications to traditional data enclave institutions, such as expanded and virtual enclaves, and of modified licens-ing arrangements for secondary data use. Direct data stewards, whether in government agencies, academic institutions, or private organizations, should participate in such research, which should seek to identify and examine the effects of various institutional mechanisms and associated enforcement systems on data access, data use, data quality, and disclosure risk.

Education and Training

RECOMMENDATION 2: Faculty, researchers, and organizations involved in the continuing professional development of researchers should engage in the education of researchers in the ethical use of spatial data. Professional associations should participate by establishing and inculcating strong norms for the ethical use and sharing of linked social-spatial data.

Education is an essential tool for ensuring that linked social-spatial data are organized and used in ways that balance the benefits of the data for developing knowledge, the value of wide access to the data, and the need to protect the confidentiality of research participants. Education and training, both for students and as part of continuing education, require materials that extrapolate from general ethical principles for data collection, maintenance, dissemination, and access. These materials should include the ethical issues raised by linked social-spatial data and, to the extent they are identified and accepted, best practices in the handling of these forms of data. Organizations and programs involved in training members of institutional review boards (IRBs) should incorporate attention to the benefits, uses, and potential risks of linked social-spatial data.

Training in Ethical Issues

RECOMMENDATION 3: Training in ethical considerations needs to accompany all methodological training in the acquisition and use of data that include geographically explicit information on research participants.

Education about how to collect, analyze, and maintain linked social-spatial data, how to disseminate results without compromising the identities of individuals involved in the research, and how to share such data consonant with confidentiality protections is essential for ensuring that scientific gains from the capacity to obtain such information can be maximized. Graduate-level courses and professional workshops addressed to ethical considerations in the conduct of research need to include attention to social and spatial data; to enhance awareness of the ethical issues related to consent, confidentiality, and benefits as well as risks of harm; and to identify the best practices available to maximize the benefits from such research while minimizing any added risks associated with explicit spatial data. Similarly, institutes, courses, and programs focusing on spatial methods and their use need to incorporate substantive consideration of ethical issues, in particular those related to confidentiality. Education needs to extend to primary and secondary researchers, staffs of organizations engaged in data dissemination, and institutional review boards (IRBs) that consider research protocols that include linked social-spatial data.

Outreach by Professional Societies and Other Organizations

RECOMMENDATION 4: Research societies and other research organizations that use linked social-spatial data and that have established traditions of protection of the confidentiality of human research participants should engage in outreach to other research societies and organizations less conversant in research with issues of human participant protection to increase their attention to these issues in the context of the use of personal, identifiable data.

Expertise on outreach is not uniformly distributed across research disciplines and fields. Given the likely increased interest in using explicit spatial data linked to other social data, funding agencies, scientific societies, and related research organizations should take steps to ensure that expertise in the conduct of research with human participants is broadly accessible and shared. An outreach priority should be to develop targeted materials, workshops, and short-course training institutes for researchers in fields or subfields that have had little or no tradition of safeguarding personal, identifiable information.

Research Design

RECOMMENDATION 5: Primary researchers who intend to collect and use spatially explicit data should design their studies in ways that not only take into account the obligation to share data and the disclosure risks posed, but also provide confidentiality protection for human participants in the primary research as well as in secondary research use of the data. Although the reconciliation of these objectives is difficult, primary researchers should nevertheless assume a significant part of this burden.

Researchers need to consider the tradeoffs between data utility and confidentiality at the very start of their research programs, when they are making commitments to sponsors, designing procedures to obtain informed consent, and presenting their plans to their IRBs. They should be mindful of both potential benefits and potential harm and plan accordingly. Everyone involved needs to understand that achieving a balance between benefits and harms may turn out to be difficult, and at the very least it will require innovative thinking, compromise, and partnership with others. It is imperative to recognize that it may take a generation to find norms for sharing the new kind of data and an equally long effort to ensure the safety of human research subjects. If, for example, IRBs need to be continuously involved in monitoring projects, they (and the researchers) should accept that role. If researchers must turn their data over to more experienced stewards for safe-keeping, that, too, will need to be acknowledged and accepted. Finally, secondary researchers need to understand that access to confidential data may involve difficulties, and plan their work accordingly.

Institutional Review Boards

RECOMMENDATION 6: Institutional Review Boards and their organizational sponsors should develop the expertise needed to make well-informed decisions that balance the objectives of data access, confidentiality, and quality in research projects that will collect or analyze linked social-spatial data.

Given the rapidity with which advances are being made in collecting and linking social and spatial data, maintaining appropriate expertise will be an ongoing task. IRBs need to learn what they do not know and develop plans to consult with experts when appropriate. Traditionally, IRBs have concerned themselves more with the collection of data than its dissemination, but the heightened risks to confidentiality that arise from linking social data to spatial data requires increased attention to data dissemination. Government agencies that sponsor research that requires the application of the common rule, the Human Subjects Research Subcommittee of the Executive Branch Committee on Research, and the Association for the Accreditation of Human Research Protection Programs (AAHRPP) should work together to convene an expert working group to address the issue of social and spatial data and make recommendations for best practices.

Data Enclaves

RECOMMENDATION 7: Data enclaves deserve further development as a way to provide wider access to high-quality data while preserving confidentiality. This development should focus on the establishment of expanded place-based enclaves, "virtual enclaves," and meaningful penalties for misuse of enclaved data.

Three elements are critical to this development. First, data producers, data stewards, and academic and other research organizations should consider expanding place-based (as opposed to virtual) data enclaves to hold more extensive collections of social and spatial data. Currently, many such data enclaves are maintained by a data producer (such as the U.S. Bureau of the Census) and contain only the data produced by that organization or agency. The panel's recommendation proposes alternative models in which organizations that store the research they produce also house social and spatial datasets produced elsewhere or in which institutions that manage multiple enclaves combine them into a single entity. This recommendation may require that some agencies (e.g., the Census Bureau) obtain regulatory or legislative approval in order to broaden their ability to manage restricted data. This approach could make such data more accessible and cost-effective for secondary researchers while also increasing the capacity and sustainability of data enclaves. The main challenge is to work out adequate confidentiality protection arrangements between data producers and the stewards of expanded enclaves.

Second, "virtual enclaves," in which data are housed in a remote location but accessed in a secure setting by researchers at their own institution under agreed rules, deserve further development. Virtual archives at academic institutions should be managed by their libraries, which have expertise in maintaining the security of valuable information resources, such as rare books and institutional archives. The Census Bureau has demonstrated the effectiveness of such remote archives with the technology used for its Research Data Centers, and Statistics Canada has created a system that is relatively more accessible (relative to the number of Canadian researchers) through its Research Data Centre program (see http://www.statcan.ca/english/rdc/index.htm). The extension of these approaches will reduce the cost of access to research data if researchers and their home institutions invest in construction and staffing and if principles of operation can be agreed on. One key issue in the management of virtual or remote enclaves is the location of the "watchful eye" that ensures that the behavior of restricted data users follows established rules. In some cases, the observer will be a remote computer or operator, while in others it will be a person working at the location where the data user is working, for example, in a college or university library.

Third, access to restricted data through virtual or place-based enclaves should be restricted to those who agree to abide by the confidentiality protections governing such data, and meaningful penalties should be enforced for willful misuse of the linked social-spatial data. High-quality science depends on sound ethical practices. Ethical standards in all fields of science require honoring agreements made as a condition of undertaking professional work—whether those agreements are between primary researchers and research participants or between researchers and research repository in the case of secondary use. Appropriate penalties might include publication of reports of willful misuse, disbarment from future research using restricted-access data, reduced access to federal research funding, and mechanisms that would provide incentives to institutions that employ researchers who willfully or carelessly misuse enclaved data so that they enforce agreements to which they are party.

Licensing

RECOMMENDATION 8: Data stewards should develop licensing agreements to provide increased access to linked social-spatial datasets that include confidential information.

Licensing agreements place the burden of confidentiality protection on the data user. Several aspects of licensing deserve further development. First, nontransferable, time-limited licenses require the data user only to ensure that his or her own use does not make respondents identifiable to others or cause them harm and to return or destroy all copies of the data as promised. However, to be effective, such agreements require strong incentives for users to protect the confidentiality of the research participants.

Second, strong licensing, which requires data users to take special precautions to protect the shared data, can make sensitive data more widely available than has been the case to date. Data stewards who are responsible for managing data enclaves or other restricted data centers, as well as research sponsors who support research that can only be disseminated under tight restrictions, should make these kinds of data as accessible as possible. Strong licensing agreements provide an appropriate mechanism for providing increased access in many situations.

Third, research planning should include mechanisms to facilitate data use under license. Sponsors of primary research should ensure that plans are developed at the outset, with sufficient resources provided (e.g., time to do research, funds to pay for access) to prepare datasets that facilitate analysis by secondary data users. Data sponsors and data stewards should ensure that the plans for data access are carried through.

Fourth, explicit enforcement language should be included in contracts and license agreements with secondary users setting forth penalties for breaches of confidentiality and other willful misuse of the linked geospatial and social data. Funding agencies and research societies with codes of ethics should scrutinize confidentiality breaches that occur and take actions appropriate to their roles and responsibilities.

References

Abowd, J.M., and J. Lane
  2003 The Economics of Data Confidentiality. Cornell University and the Urban Institute, Washington, DC. Available: http://www7.nationalacademies.org/cnstat/Abowd_Lane.pdf [accessed April 2006].
Abowd, J.M., and S.D. Woodcock
  2001 Disclosure limitation in longitudinal linked data. Pp. 216-277 in P. Doyle, J. Lane, L. Zayatz, and J. Theeuwes, eds., *Confidentiality, Disclosure, and Data Access: Theory and Practical Applications for Statistical Agencies.* Amsterdam, Netherlands: North-Holland Elsevier.
Agrawal, R., and R. Srikant
  2000 Privacy-preserving data mining. Pp. 439-450 in *Proceedings of the 2000 ACM SIGMOD on Management of Data.* New York: ACM Press.
Anderson, M., and Fienberg, S.F.
  1997 Who counts? The politics of census taking. *Society* 34(3):19-26.
Anselin, L.
  2005 Exploring Spatial Data with GeoDa™: A Workbook. Center for Spatially Integrated Social Science, University of Illinois, Urbana-Champaign. Available: http://www.geoda.uiuc.edu/pdf/geodaworkbook.pdf [accessed April 2006].
Anselin, L., I. Syabri, I., and Y. Kho
  2006 GeoDa: An introduction to spatial data analysis. *Geographical Analysis* 38(1):5-22.
Arizona State University
  2006 Central Arizona-Phoenix Long-Term Ecological Research Project, Global Institute of Sustainability. Available: http://caplter.asu.edu/home/data/index.jsp [accessed November 2006].
Armstrong, M.P., and A. Ruggles
  2005 Geographic information technologies and personal privacy. *Cartographica* 40(4):63-73.

Armstrong, M.P., G. Rushton, and D.L. Zimmerman
    1999   Geographically masking health data to preserve confidentiality. *Statistics in Medicine* 18:497-525.
Balk, D., T. Pullum, A. Storeygard, F. Greenwell, and M. Neuman
    2004   A spatial analysis of childhood mortality in West Africa. *Population, Space and Place* 10:175-216.
Balk, D., A. Storeygard, M. Levy, J. Gaskell, M. Sharma, and R. Flor
    2005   Child hunger in the developing world: An analysis of environmental and social correlates. *Food Policy* 30(5-6):584-611.
Benaloh, J.
    1987   Secret sharing homomorphisms: Keeping shares of a secret secret. Pp. 251-260 in A.M. Odlyzko, ed., *Crypto86*. Lecture Notes in Computer Science No. 263. Berlin, Germany: Springer-Verlag.
Bethlehem, J.G., W.J. Keller, and J. Pannekoek
    1990   Disclosure control of microdata. *Journal of the American Statistical Association* 85:38-45.
Bivand, R.
    2006   Implementing spatial data analysis software tools in R. *Geographical Analysis* 38(1):23-40.
Blien, U., H. Wirth, and M. Muller
    1992   Disclosure risk for microdata stemming from official statistics. *Statistica Neerlandica* 46:69-82.
Borgatti, S.P., and J.L. Molina
    2003   Ethical and strategic issues in organizational social network analysis. *The Journal of Applied Behavioral Science* 39(30):337-349.
Borriello, G., M. Chalmers, A. LaMarca, and P. Nixon
    2005   Delivering real-world ubiquitous location systems. *Communications of the Association for Computing Machinery* 48(3):36-41.
Boulos, M.N.K., Q. Cai, J.A. Padget, and G. Rushton
    2006   Using software agents to preserve individual health data confidentiality in microscale geographical analyses. *Journal of Biomedical Informatics* 39(2):160-170.
Breiger, R.L.
    2005   Introduction to special issue: Ethical dilemmas in social network research. *Social Networks* 27(2):89-93.
Brownstein, J.S., C.A. Cassa, and K.D. Mandi
    2006   No place to hide—Reverse identification of patients from published maps. *New England Journal of Medicine* 355(16):1741-1742.
Butz, W., and B.B. Torrey
    2006   Some frontiers in social science. *Science* 312:1898-1900.
Chakraborty, J., and M.P. Armstrong
    2001   Assessing the impact of airborne toxic releases on populations with special needs. *The Professional Geographer* 53:119-131.
Chawla, S., C. Dwork, F. McSherry, A. Smith, and H. Wee
    2005   Towards privacy in public databases. Pp. 363-385 in J. Kilian, ed., *Theory of Cryptography Conference Proceedings*. Lecture Notes in Computer Science 3378. Berlin, Germany: Springer-Verlag.
Chen, G., and S. Keller-McNulty
    1998   Estimation of identification disclosure risk in microdata. *Journal of Official Statistics* 14:79-95.

Churches, T., and P. Christen
    2004   Some methods for blindfolded record linkage. *BMC Medical Informatics and Decision Making* 4(9). Available: http://www.pubmedcentral.nih.gov/tocrender. fcgi?iid=10563 [accessed April 2006].

Clark, W.A.V., and K. Avery
    1976   The effects of data aggregation in statistical analysis. *Geographical Analysis* 8:428-438.

Confidentiality and Data Access Committee
    2000   Panel on Disclosure Review Boards of Federal Agencies: Characteristics, Defining Qualities, and Generalizability. 2000 Joint Statitistic Meetings, Indianapolis, IN. Available: http://www.fcsm.gov/committees/cdac/DRB-Panel.doc [accessed April 2006].
    2002   Indentifiability in Microdata Files. Available: http://www.fcsm.gov/committees/cdac/cdacra9.doc [accessed April 2006].

Cowen, D., and J.R. Jensen
    1998   Extraction and modeling of urban attributes using remote sensing. Pp. 164-188 in National Research Council, *People and Pixels: Linking Remote Sensing and Social Science.* Committee on the Human Dimensions of Global Change, D. Liverman, E.F. Moran, R.R. Rindfuss, and P.C. Stern, eds. Washington, DC: National Academy Press.

Cowen, D., J. Jensen, J. Halls, M. King, and S. Narumalani
    1993   Estimating Housing Density with CAMS Remotely Sensed Data. *Proceedings, American Congress on Surveying and Mapping/American Society for Photogrammetry and Remote Sensing* (ACRM/ASPRS):35-43.

Cox, L.H.
    1980   Suppression methodology and statistical disclosure control. *Journal of the American Statistical Association* 75:377-385.
    1995   Network models for complementary cell suppression. *Journal of the American Statistical Association* 90:1453-1462.
    1996   Protecting confidentiality in small population health and environmental statistics. *Statistics in Medicine* 15:1895-1905.
    2004   Inference control problems in statistical disclosure query systems. Pp. 1-13 in *Research Directions in Data and Applications Security*, C. Farkas and P. Samarati, eds. Boston, MA: Kluwer.

Cox, L.H., J.P. Kelly, and R. Patil
    2004   Balancing quality and confidentiality for multivariate tabular data. Pp. 87-98 in J. Domingo-Ferrer and V. Torra, eds., *Privacy in Statistical Databases.* Lecture Notes in Computer Science, vol. 3050. Berlin, Germany: Springer-Verlag.

Culler, D., D. Estrin, and M. Srivastava
    2004   Overview of sensor networks. *Computer* 37(8):41-49.

Dale, A., and M. Elliot
    2001   Proposals for 2001 samples of anonymized records: an assessment of disclosure risk. *Journal of the Royal Statistical Society, Series A* 164:427-447.

Deane, G.D., and M.P. Gutmann
    2003   Blowin' down the road: Investigating bilateral causality between dust storms and population change in the Great Plains. *Population Research and Policy Review* 22:297-331.

de Wolf, V.
    2003   Issues in accessing and sharing confidential survey and social science data. *Data Science Journal* 2 (17 Feb):66-74.

Dobson, J.E., and P.F. Fisher
    2003   Geoslavery. *Technology and Society* 22(1):47-52.

Domingo-Ferrer, J., and V. Torra
    2001   A quantitative comparison of disclosure control methods for microdata. Pp.
            111-133 in P. Doyle, J. Lane, L. Zayatz, and J. Theeuwes, eds., *Disclosure, and
            Data Access: Theory and Practical Applications.* Amsterdam, Netherlands:
            North-Holland Elsevier.
Doyle P., J. I. Lane, J.J.M. Theeuwe, and L.V. Zayatz, eds.
    2002   *Confidentiality, Disclosure and Data Access: Theory and Practical Applications
            for Statistical Agencies.* Amsterdam, Netherlands: North-Holland Elsevier.
Duncan, G.T., and D. Lambert
    1986a   Disclosure-limited data dissemination. *Journal of the American Statistical Asso-
            ciation* 81:10-28.
    1986b   The risk of disclosure for microdata. *Journal of Business and Economic Statistics*
            7:207-217.
Duncan, G.T., S.A. Keller-McNulty, and S.L. Stokes
    2001   Disclosure Risk vs. Data Utility: The R-U Confidentiality Map. Technical Re-
            port, U.S. National Institute of Statistical Sciences, Research Triangle Park, NC.
Electronic Privacy Information Center
    2003   *The Census and Privacy.* Available: http://www.epic.org/privacy/census/ [ac-
            cessed July 2006].
Entwisle, B., R.R. Rindfuss, S.J. Walsh, T.P. Evans, and S.R. Curran
    1997   Geographic information systems, spatial network analysis, and contraceptive
            choice. *Demography* 34:171-187.
Federal Committee on Statistical Methodology
    1994   Statistical Policy Working Paper 22: Report on Statistical Disclosure Limitation
            Methodology. Subcommittee on Disclosure Limitation Methodology, Office of
            Management and Budget, Executive Office of the President. Washington, DC:
            U.S. General Printing Office.
Fienberg, S.E., and U.E. Makov
    1998   Confidentiality, uniqueness, and disclosure limitation for categorical data. *Jour-
            nal of Official Statistics* 14:361-372.
Fienberg, S.E., U.E. Makov, and A.P. Sanil
    1997   A Bayesian approach to data disclosure: Optimal intruder behavior for continu-
            ous data. *Journal of Official Statistics* 13:75-89.
Fienberg, S.E., and A.B. Slavkovic
    2004   Making the release of confidential data from multi-way tables count. *Chance*
            17(3):5-10.
    2005   Preserving the confidentiality of categorical statistical data bases when releasing
            information for association rules. *Data Mining and Knowledge Discovery* 11:
            155-180.
Fisher, P., and J. Dobson
    2003   Who knows where you are, and who should, in the era of mobile geography?
            Geography 88:331-337.
Foster, A.
    2005   A review of ten years of work on economic growth and population change in
            rural India. Pp. 287-308 in National Research Council, *Population, Land Use,
            and Environment: Research Directions.* Panel on New Research on Population
            and the Environment, B. Entwisle and P.C. Stern, eds. Washington, DC: The
            National Academies Press.
Fotheringham, A.S., C. Brunsdon, and M. Charlton
    2002   *Geographically Weighted Regression.* Hoboken, NJ: John Wiley & Sons.
Fuller, W.A.
    1993   Masking procedures for microdata disclosure limitation. *Journal of Official Sta-
            tistics* 9:383-406.

Geer, D.
    2006   Nanotechnology: The growing impact of shrinking computers. *Pervasive Computing* 5:7-11.

Gephart, M.A.
    1997   Neighborhoods and communities as contexts for development. Pp. 1-43 in J. Brooks-Gunn, G.J. Duncan, and J.L. Aber, eds., *Neighborhood Poverty: Context and Consequences for Children*. New York: Russell Sage.

Gomatam, S., A.F. Karr, J.P Reiter, and A.P. Sanil
    2005   Data dissemination and disclosure limitation in a world without microdata: A risk-utility framework for remote access servers. *Statistical Science* 20:163-177.

Gordon-Larsen, P., M.C. Nelson, P. Page, and B.M. Popkin
    2006   Inequality in the built environment underlies key health disparities in physical activity and obesity. *Pediatrics* 117:417-424.

Goss, J.
    1995   We know who you are and we know where you live: The instrumental rationality of geodemographic systems. *Economic Geography* 71:171-198.

Greenberg, B., and L.V. Zayatz
    1992   Strategies for measuring risk in public use microdata files. *Statistica Neerlandica* 46:33-48.

Gutmann, M.P., G.D. Deane, N. Lauster, and A. Peri
    2006   Heat, elevation, and migration: Two population-environment regimes in the Great Plains of the United States, 1930-1990. *Population and Environment* 27(2):191-225. Available: http://www.springerlink.com/content/f51434802p 621653/ [accessed December 2006].

Hutchinson, C.F.
    1998   Social science and remote sensing in famine early warning. Pp. 189-196 in National Research Council, *People and Pixels: Linking Remote Sensing and Social Science*. Committee on the Human Dimensions of Global Change, D. Liverman, F.F. Moran, R.R. Rindfuss, and P.C. Stern, eds. Washington, DC: National Academy Press.

Indiana University
    2006   Anthropological Center for Training and Research on Global Environmental Change. Available: http://www.indiana.edu/%7Eact/research.htm [accessed November 2006].

Inter-university Consortium for Political and Social Research
    2005   Guide to Social Science Data Preparation and Archiving. Third Edition. Available: http://www.icpsr.umich.edu/access/dataprep.pdf [accessed April 2006].

Jabine, T.B.
    1993   Statistical disclosure limitation practices of United States statistical agencies. *Journal of Official Statistics* 9:427-454.

Kadushin, C.
    2005   Who benefits from network analysis: Ethics of social network research. *Social Networks* 27(2):139-153.

Karr, A.F., X. Lin, A.P. Sanil, and J.P. Reiter
    2005   Secure regressions on distributed databases. *Journal of Computational and Graphical Statistics* 14:263-279.

Kennickell, A.B.
    1997   Multiple imputation and disclosure protection: The case of the 1995 survey of consumer finances. Pp. 248-267 in National Research Council, *Record Linkage Techniques*. Committee on Applied and Theoretical Statistics. Washington, DC: National Academy Press.

Klovdahl, A.S.
    2005   Social network research and human subjects protection: Towards more effective infectious disease control. *Social Networks* 27(2):119-137.
Kwan, M.-P.
    2003   Individual accessibility revisited: Implications for geographical analysis in the twenty-first century. *Geographical Analysis* 35(4):341-353.
Lahlou, S., M. Langheinrich, and C. Röcker
    2005   Privacy and trust issues with invisible computers. *Communications of the Association for Computing Machinery* 48(3):59-60.
Lambert, D.
    1993   Measures of disclosure risk and harm. *Journal of Official Statistics* 9:313-331.
LeClere, F.B., R.G. Rogers, and K.D. Peters
    1998   Neighborhood social context and racial differences in women's heart disease mortality. *Journal of Health and Social Behavior* 39:91-107.
Levine, F., and P.R. Skedsvold
    2006   Behavioral and social science research. In E.J. Emanuel, R.A. Crouch, C. Grady, R. Lie, F. Miller, and D. Wendler, eds., *The Oxford Textbook of Clinical Research Ethics.* Oxford, England: Oxford University Press.
Little, R.J.A.
    1993   Statistical analysis of masked data. *Journal of Official Statistics* 9:407-426.
Martinez, K., J.K. Hart, and R. Ong
    2004   Environmental sensor networks. *Computer* 37(8):50-56.
McGrahanan, G., P. Marcotullio, X. Bai, D. Balk, T. Braga, I. Douglas, T. Elmqvist, W. Rees, D. Satterthwaite, J. Songsore, and H. Zlotnik
    2005   Urban systems. Chapter 22 in *Conditions and Trends Assessment of the Millennium Ecosystem Assessment.* Chicago, IL: Island Press.
McGranahan, G., D. Balk, and B. Anderson
    2006   Low coastal zone settlements. *Tiempo: A Bulletin on Climate and Development* 59(April):23-26.
Melichar, L., J. Evans, and C. Bachrach
    2002   Data Access and Archiving: Options for the Demographic and Behavioral Sciences Branch. Deliberations and Recommendations of DBSB Workshop. Available: http://www.nichd.nih.gov/publications/pubs/upload/data_access.pdf [accessed November 2006].
Minnesota Population Center, University of Minnesota, and Inter-university Consortium for Political and Social Research Census 2000 Advisory Committee
    2000   The Public Use Microdata Samples of the U.S. Census: Research Applications and Privacy Issues. Census. 2000 Users' Conference on PUMS, Alexandria, VA. Available: http://www.pop.umn.edu/~census2000/index_older.html [accessed July 2006].
Monmonier, M.
    2002   *Spying with Maps: Surveillance Technologies and the Future of Privacy.* Chicago, IL: The University of Chicago Press.
Moran, E.F., E.S. Brondizio, and L.K. VanWey
    2005   Population and Environment in Amazonia: Landscape and household dynamics. Pp. 106-134 in National Research Council, *Population, Land Use, and Environment: Research Directions.* Panel on New Research on Population and the Environment, B. Entwisle and P.C. Stern, eds. Washington, DC: The National Academies Press.

National Center for Health Statistics and Centers for Disease Control and Prevention
    2003   Zip Code Tabulation Area and Confidentiality. Joint ECE/Eurostat Work Session on Statistical Data Confidentiality, Conference of European Statisticians, Luxembourg, 7-9 April 2003, sponsored by United Nations Statistical Commission and Economic Commission for Europe and European Commission, Statistical Office of the European Communities (EUROSTAT). Available: http://www.unece.org/stats/documents/2003/04/confidentiality/wp.34.e.pdf [accessed April 2006].

National Commission for the Protection of Human Subjects of Biomedical and Behavioral Research
    1979   *Belmont Report: Ethical Principles and Guidelines for the Protection of Human Subjects of Research.* GPO 887-809. Washington. DC: U.S. Government Printing Office.

National Research Council
    1985   *Sharing Research Data.* Committee on National Statistics, S. Fienberg, L. Martin, and M. Straf, eds. Washington, DC: National Academy Press.
    1993   *Private Lives and Public Policies: Confidentiality and Accesssibility of Government Statistics.* Panel on Confidentiality and Data Access, Committee on National Statistics, G.T. Duncan, T.B. Jabine, and V.A. deWolf, eds. Washington, DC: National Academy Press.
    1998   *People and Pixels: Linking Remote Sensing and Social Science.* Committee on the Human Dimensions of Global Change, D. Liverman, F.F. Moran, R.R. Rindfuss, and P.C. Stern, eds. Washington, DC: National Academy Press.
    2000   *Improving Access to and Confidentiality of Research Data: Report of a Workshop.* Committee on National Statistics, C. Mackie and N. Bradburn, eds. Washington, DC: National Academy Press.
    2001   *Resolving Conflicts Arising from the Privatization of Environmental Data.* Committee on Geophysical and Environmental Data, Board on Earth Sciences and Resources, Division on Earth and Life Studies. Washington, DC: National Academy Press.
    2003   *Access to Research Data in the 21st Century: An Ongoing Dialogue Among Interested Parties.* Science, Technology, and Law Panel, Division of Policy and Global Affairs. Washington, DC: The National Academies Press.
    2004a *Licensing Geographic Data and Services.* Committee on Licensing Geographic Data and Services, Board on Earth Sciences and Resources. Washington, DC: The National Academies Press.
    2004b *Protecting Participants and Facilitating Social and Behavioral Science Research.* Panel on Institutional Review Boards, Surveys, and Social Science Research, C.F. Citro, D.R. Ilgen, and C.B. Marrett, eds., Committee on National Statistics and Board on Behavioral, Cognitive and Sensory Sciences. Washington, DC: The National Academies Press.
    2005a *Expanding Access to Research Data: Reconciling Risks and Opportunities.* Panel on Data Access for Research Purposes, Committee on National Statistics: Washington, DC: The National Academies Press.
    2005b *Population, Land Use, and Environment: Research Directions.* Panel on New Research on Population and the Environment, B. Entwisle and P.C. Stern, eds. Washington, DC: The National Academies Press.

New York Times
    2006   House panel to press cellphone industry on improving protection of customer records. February 1:C3 (late edition). Available: http://select.nytimes.com/search/restricted/article?res=F70F11FF345B0C728CDDAB0894DE404482 [accessed April 2006].

O'Harrow, R.
    2005   *No Place to Hide.* New York: Free Press.
O'Keefe, C.M., M. Yung, L. Gu, and R. Baxter
    2004   Privacy-preserving data linkage protocols. Pp. 94-102 in V. Atluri, P. Syverson, and S. De Capitani di Vimercati, eds. *Proceedings of the 2004 ACM Workshop on Privacy in the Electronic Society, WPES 2004.* Washington, DC: ACM Press.
Openshaw, S., and P.J. Taylor
    1979   A million or so correlation coefficients: Three experiments on the modifiable areal unit problem. Pp. 127-144 in N. Wrigley, ed., *Statistical Applications in the Spatial Sciences.* London, England: Pion.
Paass, G.
    1988   Disclosure risk and disclosure avoidance for microdata. *Journal of Business and Economic Statistics* 6:487-500.
Pannekoek, J.
    1999   Statistical methods for some simple disclosure limitation rules. *Statistica Neerlandica* 53:55-67.
Parker, E.B.
    1998   Measuring access to primary medical care: some examples of the use of geographical information systems. *Health and Place* 4(2):183-193.
Raghunathan, T.E., J.M. Lepkowski, J. van Hoewyk, and P. Solenberger
    2001   A multivariate technique for multiply imputing missing values using a series of regression models. *Survey Methodology* 27:85-96.
Raghunathan, T.E., J.P. Reiter, and D.B. Rubin
    2003   Multiple imputation for statistical disclosure limitation. *Journal of Official Statistics* 19:1-16.
Reiter, J.P.
    2002   Satisfying disclosure restrictions with synthetic data sets. *Journal of Official Statistics* 18:531-544.
    2003   Inference for partially synthetic, public use microdata sets. *Survey Methodology* 29:181-189.
    2004   Simultaneous use of multiple imputation for missing data and disclosure limitation. *Survey Methodology* 30:235-242.
    2005a Estimating risks of identification disclosure in microdata. *Journal of the American Statistical Association* 100:1103-1113.
    2005b Releasing multiply-imputed, synthetic public use microdata: An illustration and empirical study. *Journal of the Royal Statistical Society, Series A*:168, 185-205.
    2005c Significance tests for multi-component estimands from multiply-imputed, synthetic microdata. *Journal of Statistical Planning and Inference* 131:365-377.
    2005d Using CART to generate partially synthetic, public use microdata. *Journal of Official Statistics* 21:441-462.
Robinson, W.S.
    1950   Ecological correlation and the behavior of individuals. *American Sociological Review* 15:351-357.
Ross, C.E., J.R. Reynolds, and K.J. Geis
    2000   The contingent meaning of neighborhood stability for residents' psychological well-being. *American Sociological Review* 65:581-595.
Rubin, D.B.
    1993   Discussion: Statistical disclosure limitation. *Journal of Official Statistics* 9:462-468.

Rushton, G., M.P. Armstrong, J. Gittler, B. Greene, C.E. Pavlik, M. West, M. and D. Zimmerman
    2006   Geocoding in cancer research: A review. *American Journal of Preventive Medicine* 30(2, Suppl. 1):S16-S24.
Sampson, R.J., J.D. Morenoff, and T. Gannon-Rowley
    2002   Assessing 'neighborhood effects': Social processes and new directions in research. *Annual Review of Sociology* 28:443-478.
Samuels, S.M.
    1998   A Bayesian species-sampling-inspired approach to the unique problems in microdata. *Journal of Official Statistics* 14:373-384.
Seastrom, M.M.
    2002   Licensing. Pp. 279-296 in *Confidentiality, Disclosure and Data Access: Theory and Practical Applications for Statistical Agencies*, P. Doyle, J. Lane, J.J.M. Theeuwes, and L. Zayatz, eds. Amsterdam, Netherlands: North-Holland Elsevier.
Seto, K.C.
    2005   Economies, societies, and landscapes in transition: Examples from the Pearl River Delta, China, and the Red River Delta, Vietnam. Pp. 193-216 in National Research Council, *Population, Land Use, and Environment: Research Directions*. Panel on New Research on Population and the Environment, B. Entwisle and P.C. Stern, eds. Washington, DC: The National Academies Press.
Skinner, C.J.
    1992   On identification disclosure and prediction disclosure for microdata. *Statistica Neerlandica* 46:21-32.
Skinner, C.J., and M.J. Elliot
    2002   A measure of disclosure risk for microdata. *Journal of the Royal Statistical Society, Series B* 64:855-867.
Skinner, C., C. Marsh, S. Openshaw, and C. Wymer
    1994   Disclosure control for census microdata. *Journal of Official Statistics* 10:31-51.
Smailagic, A., and D.P. Siewiorek
    2002   Application design for wearable and context-aware computers. *Pervasive Computing* 1(4):20-29.
Small, C., and J.E. Cohen
    2004   Continental physiography, climate, and the global distribution of human population. *Current Anthropology* 45(2):269-277.
Small, C., and R.J. Nicholls
    2003   A global analysis of human settlement in coastal zones. *Journal of Coastal Research* 19(3):584-599.
Smith, K.R., and N.J. Waitzman
    1997   Effects of marital status on the risk of mortality in poor and non-poor neighborhoods. *Annals of Epidemiology* 7:343-349.
Spruill, N.L.
    1982   Measures of confidentiality. Pp. 260-265 in *Proceedings of the Section on Survey Research Methods of the American Statistical Association*. Alexandria, VA: American Statistical Association.
Streitz, N., and P. Nixon
    2005   The disappearing computer. *Communications of the Association for Computing Machinery* 48(3):33-35.
Sui, D.
    2005   Will ubicomp make GIS invisible? *Computers, Environment and Urban Systems* 29:361-367.

80 PUTTING PEOPLE ON THE MAP

University of Michigan
2005a Project SLUCE: Spatial Land Use Change and Ecological Effects at the Rural-Urban Interface: Agent-Based Modeling and Evaluation of Alternative Policies and Interventions. Available: http://www.cscs.umich.edu/sluce [accessed April 2006].
2005b Reciprocal Relations Between Population and Environment Project, Population Studies Center. Available: http://www.psc.isr.umich.edu/research/project-detail.html?ID=51 [accessed April 2006].
University of North Carolina
2005 Ecuador Projects, Carolina Population Center. Available: http://www.cpc.unc.edu/projects/Ecuador [accessed November 2006].
2006 Nang Rong Projects, Carolina Population Center: Available: http://www.cpc.unc.edu/projects/nangrong [accessed November 2006].
VanWey, L.K., Rindfuss, R.R., Gutmann, M.P., Entwisle, B.E., and Balk, D.L.
2005 Confidentiality and spatially explicit data: Concerns and challenges. *Proceedings of the National Academy of Sciences* 102:15337-15342.
Walsh, S.J., R.R. Rindfuss, P. Prasartkul, B. Entwisle, and A. Chamratrithirong
2005 Population change and landscape dynamics: The Nang Rong, Thailand studies. Pp. 135-162 in National Research Council, *Population, Land Use, and Environment: Research Directions.* Panel on New Research on Population and the Environment, B. Entwisle and P.C. Stern, eds. Washington, DC: The National Academies Press.
Want, R.
2006 An introduction to RFID technology. *Pervasive Computing* 5(1):25-33.
Weeks, J.R., D.P. Larson, and D.L. Fugate
2005 Patterns of urban land use as assessed by satellite imagery: An application to Cairo, Egypt. Pp. 265-286 in National Research Council *Population, Land Use, and Environment: Research Directions.* Panel on New Research on Population and the Environment, B. Entwisle and P.C. Stern, eds. Washington, DC: The National Academies Press.
Weiser, M.
1991 The computer for the 21st century. *Scientific American* 265(3):94-104.
Willenborg, L., and T. de Waal
1996 *Statistical Disclosure Control in Practice.* New York: Springer-Verlag.
2001 *Elements of Statistical Disclosure Control.* New York: Springer-Verlag.
Williams, A.P.
1983 How many miles to the doctor? *The New England Journal of Medicine* 309(16):958-963.
Wood, C.H., and D. Skole
1998 Linking satellite, census, and survey data to study deforestation in the Brazilian Amazon. Pp. 70-93 in National Research Council, *People and Pixels: Linking Remote Sensing and Social Science.* Committee on the Human Dimensions of Global Change, D. Liverman, F.F. Moran, R.R. Rindfuss, and P.C. Stern, eds. Washington, DC: National Academy Press.
Yancey, W.E., W.E. Winkler, and R.H. Creecy
2002 Disclosure risk assessment in perturbative microdata protection. In J. Domingo-Ferrer, ed., *Inference Control in Statistical Databases.* Berlin, Germany: Springer-Verlag.

Apppendix A

Privacy for Research Data

Robert Gellman

INTRODUCTION

Scope and Purpose

The purpose of this paper is to describe privacy rules in the three most important areas relevant to research uses of information involving remotely sensed and self-identifying data. The three issues are (1) When is information sufficiently identifiable so that privacy rules apply or privacy concerns attach? (2) When does the collection of personal information fall under regulation? and (3) What rules govern the disclosure of personal information? In addition, a short discussion of liability for improper use or disclosure is included. The goal is to provide sufficient information to illustrate where lines—albeit vague, inconsistent, and incomplete—have been drawn.

Spatial information can have a variety of relationships with personal data. A home address is spatial information that is likely to be personally identifiable and will typically be included within the scope of statutory privacy protections along with name, number, and other personal data. Even in the absence of a statute, spatial data that are identifiable raise overt privacy issues. In other contexts, spatial information linked with otherwise nonidentifiable personal data (e.g., from an anonymous survey) may produce data that are personally identifiable or that may be potentially personally identifiable. Spatial information is not unique in being either identifiable or linkable. However, the manner in which spatial information can become linked with identifiable data or may create identifiable data differs in practice from that for other types of data in both overt and subtle ways.

In general, data about individuals are growing more identifiable as more information is collected, maintained, and available for public and private uses. Technological developments also contribute to the increasing identifiability of data that do not have overt identifiers. Spatial information has both of these characteristics, more data and better technology. Linking spatial information to research data can affect promises of confidentiality that were made at the time of data collection and in ways that were not foreseeable at that time. These are some of the challenges presented by the use of spatial information.

Two preliminary observations about the complexity of privacy regulation are in order. First, privacy regulation can be highly variable and unpredictable in application. In the United States, privacy standards established by statute may differ depending on the extent to which the information is identifiable, the type of information, the identity of the record keeper, the identity of the user, the purpose for which the information was collected or is being used, the type of technology employed, and other elements. For some information activities, such as surveillance, additional factors may be relevant, including the manner in which information is stored or transmitted, the location being surveilled, the place from which the surveillance is done, and the nationality of the target. This list of factors is not exhaustive.

Second, American privacy regulation is often nonexistent. Privacy statutes are often responsive to widely reported horror stories, and there are huge gaps in statutory protections for privacy. For many types of personal information, many categories of record keepers, and many types of information collection and disclosure activities, no privacy rules apply. Furthermore, where regulation exists, information can sometimes be transferred from a regulated to a nonregulated environment. A person in possession of information regulated for privacy may be able to disclose the information to a third party who is beyond the regulatory scheme. Common law standards may apply at times, but they rarely provide clear guidance.

The paper begins by discussing terminology, particularly distinctions between privacy and confidentiality, and considers privacy as it is addressed in legislation, administrative process, professional standards, and litigation in the United States. Major legal and policy issues considered are identifiability of personal data, data collection limitations, disclosure rules, and liability for misuse of data.

A Note on Terminology

Privacy and *confidentiality* are troublesome terms because neither has a universally recognized definition. While broad definitions can be found, none is enlightening because definitions are at too high a level of abstraction and never offer operational guidance applicable in all contexts. Nevertheless, because the terms are impossible to avoid, some clarification is appropriate.

Privacy is generally an attribute of individuals. While some foreign laws grant privacy rights to legal persons (e.g., corporations) as well as individuals, American usage usually ties privacy interests to individuals. That usage will be followed in this paper.

The scope of privacy interests that should be recognized is much debated. Philosophers, sociologists, economists, physicians, lawyers, and others have different views on the goals and meaning of privacy protection. For present purposes, however, the focus is primarily on the privacy of personal information. Europeans and others refer to this aspect of privacy as data protection.

The most universally recognized statement of information privacy policy comes from a 1980 document about Fair Information Practices (FIPs) from the Organisation for Economic Co-Operation and Development.[1] While this statement is not free from controversy, FIPs provide a highly useful framework for discussing and evaluating information privacy matters. FIPs are useful because the principles define the elements of privacy in some detail, and the details are crucial. The implementation of FIPs in any context will vary because the principles are broad and not self-executing. Applying FIPs is as much art as science.

Confidentiality is an attribute that can apply to individuals and to legal persons. Both personal information and business information may be confidential. However, the precise meaning of that designation is often unclear. Statutes often designate information with the single-word descriptor of confidential. However, these laws routinely fail to define the scope of confidentiality, the obligations of record keepers, or the rights of record subjects or third parties. Those who maintain statutorily designated confidential records may have to decide on their own if they can disclose information to contractors, to police, to researchers, when required by other statutes, in response to a subpoena, when requested by the data subject, or otherwise. Standards for data collection, security, data quality, accountability, or access and correction rights are typically wholly unaddressed.

Statutes that protect business information from disclosure suffer from the same lack of specificity. The federal Freedom of Information Act (FOIA) allows agencies to withhold "trade secrets and commercial or financial information obtained from a person and privileged or confidential."[2] Each of the terms in this phrase has been the subject of litigation, and different courts have reached significantly different interpretations of what constitutes confidential business information.

Categories of data held by government agencies sometimes have a designation suggesting or imposing a degree of secrecy. Under the Executive Order on Security Classification,[3] *confidential* is one of three terms with a defined scope and process for designation of information that requires protection in the interests of national defense and foreign policy. The other terms are *secret* and *top secret*. However, many other terms used by federal agencies (e.g., "for official use only" or "sensitive but unclassified") to categorize information as having some degree of confidentiality have no defined standards.

The term *confidential* is much harder to encircle with a definition, whether in whole or in part. It retains a useful meaning as broadly descriptive of information of any type that may not be appropriate for unrestricted public disclosure. Unadorned, however, a confidential designation cannot be taken as a useful descriptor of rights and responsibilities. It offers a sentiment and not a standard.

The terms *privacy* and *confidentiality* will not, by themselves, inform anyone of the proper way to process information or balance the interests of the parties to information collection, maintenance, use, or disclosure. In any context, the propriety and legality of any type of information processing must be judged by legal standards when applicable or by other standards, be they ethical, social, or local.

Local standards may arise from promises made by those who collect and use personal data. Standards may be found, for example, in website privacy policies or in promises made by researchers as part of the informed consent process. In nearly all cases, broad promises of confidentiality may create expectations that record keepers may not be able to fulfill. The laws that may allow or require disclosure of records to third parties—and particularly the federal government—create a reality that cannot be hidden behind a general promise of confidentiality. Other aspects of privacy (i.e., FIPs) may also require careful delineation. The vagueness of commonly used terminology increases the need for clarity and specificity.

IDENTIFIABILITY AND PRIVACY

Information privacy laws protect personal privacy interests by regulating the collection, maintenance, use, and disclosure of personal information. The protection of identifiable individuals is a principal goal of these laws.[4] Usually, it is apparent when information relates to an identifiable individual because it includes a name, address, identification number, or other overt identifier associated with a specific individual. Personal information that cannot be linked to a specific individual typically falls outside the scope of privacy regulation. However, the line between the regulated and the unregulated is not always clear.

Removing overt identifiers does not ensure that the remaining information is no longer identifiable. Data not expressly associated with a specific individual may nevertheless be linked to that individual under some conditions. It may not always be easy to predict in advance when deidentified[5] data can be linked. Factors that affect the identifiability of information about individuals include unique or unusual data elements; the number of available nonunique data elements about the data subject; specific knowledge about the data subject already in the possession of an observer; the size of the population that includes the data subject; the amount of time and effort that an observer is willing to devote to the identification effort; and the volume of identifiable information about the population that includes the subject of the data.

In recent decades, the volume of generally available information about individuals has expanded greatly. Partly because of an absence of general privacy laws, the United States is the world leader in the commercial collection, compilation, and exploitation of personal data. American marketers and data brokers routinely combine identifiable public records (e.g., voter registers, occupational licenses, property ownership and tax records, court records), identifiable commercial data (e.g., transaction information), and nonidentifiable data (e.g., census data). They use the data to create for nearly every individual and household a profile that includes name, address, telephone number, educational level, homeownership, mail buying propensity, credit card usage, income level, marital status, age, children, and lifestyle indicators that show whether an individual is a gardener, reader, golfer, etc.[6] Records used for credit purposes are regulated by the Fair Credit Reporting Act,[7] but other consumer data compilations are mostly unregulated for privacy. As the amount of available personal data increases, it becomes less likely that nonidentifiable data will remain nonidentifiable. Latanya Sweeney, a noted expert on identifiability, has said: "I can never guarantee that any release of data is anonymous, even though for a particular user it may very well be anonymous."[8]

For the statistician or researcher, identifiability of personal data is rarely a black and white concept. Whether a set of data is identifiable can depend on the characteristics of the set itself, on factors wholly external to the set, or on the identity of the observer. Data that cannot be identified by one person may be identifiable by another, perhaps because of different skills or because of access to different information sources. Furthermore, identifiability is not a static characteristic. Data not identifiable today may be identifiable tomorrow because of developments remote from the original source of the data or the current holder of the data. As the availability of geospatial and other information increases, the ability to link wholly nonidentifiable data or deidentified data with specific individuals will also increase.

From a legislative perspective, however, identifiability is more likely to be a black and white concept. Privacy legislation tends to provide express regulation for identifiable data and nonregulation for nonidentifiable data, without any recognition of a middle ground. However, statutes do not yet generally reflect a sophisticated understanding of the issues. Until recently, policy makers outside the statistical community paid relatively little attention to the possibility of reidentification. Nevertheless, a selective review of laws and rules illustrates the range of policy choices to date.

U.S. Legislative Standards

The Privacy Act of 1974,[9] a U.S. law applicable mostly to federal agencies, defines *record* to mean a grouping of information about an individual that contains "his name, or the identifying number, symbol, or other identifying particular assigned to the individual, such as a finger or voice print or a photograph."[10] An identifier is an essential part of a record. The ability to infer identity or to reidentify a record is not sufficient or relevant.

A location may or may not be an identifier under the Privacy Act. A home address associated with a name is unquestionably an identifier. A home address without any other data element could be an identifier if only one individual lives at the address, but it might not be if more than one individual lives there. As data elements are added to the address, the context may affect whether the information is an identifier and whether the act applies. If the information associated with the address is about the property ("2,000 square feet"), then the information is probably not identifying information about an individual. If the information is about the resident ("leaves for work every day at 8:00 a.m."), it is more likely to be found to be identifying information. Part of the uncertainty here is that there is a split in the courts about how to interpret the act's concept of what is personal information. The difference does not relate specifically to location information, and the details are not enlightening.

However, the question of when a location qualifies as an identifier is an issue that could arise outside the narrow and somewhat loosely drafted Privacy Act of 1974.[11] If a location is unassociated with an individual, then it is less likely to raise a privacy issue. However, it may be possible to associate location information with an individual, so that the addition of location data to other nonidentifiable data elements may make it easier to identify a specific individual.

Other federal laws are generally unenlightening on identifiability questions. Neither the Driver's Privacy Protection Act[12] nor the Video Privacy Protection Act[13] addresses identifiability in any useful way. The Cable Communications Policy Act excludes from its definition of *personally identifiable information* "any record of aggregate data which does not identify particular persons."[14] This exclusion, which probably addressed a political issue rather than a statistical one, raises as many questions as it answers.

Congress took a more sophisticated approach to identifiability in the Confidential Information Protection and Statistical Efficiency Act of 2002 (CIPSEA).[15] The law defines *identifiable form* to mean "any representation of information that permits the identity of the respondent to whom the information applies to be reasonably inferred by either direct or indirect means." This language is probably the result of the involvement of the statistical community in the development of the legislation. The standard is a reasonableness standard, and some international examples of reasonableness standards will be described shortly. CIPSEA's definition recognizes the possibility of using indirect inferences to permit identification, but it does not indicate the scope of effort that is necessary to render deidentified data identifiable. That may be subsumed within the overall concept of reasonableness.

No Standard

National privacy laws elsewhere do not always include guidance about identifiability. Canada's Personal Information Protection and Electronic Documents Act (PIPEDA) defines personal information as "information about an identifiable individual."[16] The act includes no standard for determining identifiability or anonymity, and it does not address the issue of reidentification. A treatise on the act suggests that "caution should be exercised in determining what is truly 'anonymous' information since the availability of external information in automated format may facilitate the reidentification of information that has been made anonymous."[17]

Strict Standard

The 1978 French data protection law defines information as "nominative" if in any way it directly or indirectly permits the identification of a natural person.[18] According to an independent analysis, "the French law makes no distinction between information that can easily be linked to an individual and information that can only be linked with extraordinary means or with the cooperation of third parties."[19] The French approach does not appear to recognize any intermediate possibility between identifiable and anonymous. Unless personal data in France are wholly nonidentifiable, they appear to remain fully subject to privacy rules. This approach may provide greater clarity, but the results could be harsh in practice if data only theoretically identifiable fall under the regulatory scheme for personal data. However, the French data protection law includes several provisions that appear to ameliorate the potentially harsh results.[20]

Reasonableness Standards

The definition of *personal data* in the European Union (EU) Data Protection Directive refers to an identifiable natural person as "an individual person . . . who can be identified, directly or indirectly."[21] On the surface, the EU definition appears to be similar to the strict standard in French law. However, the directive's introductory Recital 26 suggests a softer intent when it states that privacy rules will not apply to "data rendered anonymous in such a way that the data subject is no longer identifiable." It also provides that "to determine whether a person is identifiable, account should be taken of all the means likely reasonably to be used either by the controller or by any other person to identify the said person."[22] Thus, the directive offers a reasonableness standard for determining whether data have been adequately deidentified.

Variations on a reasonableness standard can be found elsewhere. The Council of Europe's recommendations on medical data privacy provide that an individual is not identifiable "if identification requires an unreasonable amount of time and manpower."[23] An accompanying explanatory memorandum says that costs are no longer a reliable criterion for determining identifiability because of developments in computer technology.[24] However, it is unclear why "time and manpower" are not just a proxy for costs.

The Australian Privacy Act defines *personal information* to mean "information . . . about an individual whose identity is apparent, or can reasonably be ascertained, from the information."[25] It appears on the surface that a decision about identifiability is limited to determinations from the information itself and not from other sources. This language highlights the general question of just what activities and persons are included within the scope of a reasonableness determination inquiry. Under the EU directive, it is clear that identification action taken by any person is relevant. The Council of Europe uses a time and manpower measure, but without defining who might make the identification effort. The Australian law appears to limit the question to inferences from the information itself. The extent to which these differences are significantly different in application or intent is not clear.

The British Data Protection Act's definition of personal data covers data about an individual who can be identified thereby or through "other information which is in the possession of, or is likely to come into the possession of, the data controller."[26] The British standard does not expressly rely on reasonableness or on the effort required to reidentify data. It bases an identifiability determination more narrowly by focusing on information that a data controller has or is likely to acquire. This appears to be only a step removed from an express reasonableness test.

The Canadian Institutes of Health Research (CIHR) proposed a clarification of the definition of personal information from PIPEDA that may offer the most specific example of a reasonableness standard.[27] The CIHR language refers to "a reasonably foreseeable method" of identification or linking of data with a specific individual. It also refers to anonymized information "permanently stripped" of all identifiers such that the information has "no reasonable potential for any organization to make an identification." In addition, the CIHR proposal provides that reasonably foreseeability shall "be assessed with regard to the circumstances prevailing at the time of the proposed collection, use or disclosure."

Administrative Process

The Alberta Health Information Act takes a different approach. It defines *individually identifying* to mean when a data subject "can be readily ascertained from the information,"[28] and it defines *nonidentifying* to mean that the identity of the data subject "cannot be readily ascertained from the information."[29] This appears to limit the identifiability inquiry to the information itself.

Alberta's innovation comes in its regulation of data matching,[30] which is the creation of individually identifying health information by combining individually identifying or nonidentifying health information or other information from two or more electronic databases without the consent of the data subjects. The data matching requirements, which attach to anyone attempting to reidentify nonidentifying health information, include submission of a privacy impact assessment to the commissioner for review and comment.[31]

The Alberta law is different because it expressly addresses reidentification activities by anyone (at least, anyone using any electronic databases). In place of a fixed standard for determining whether identifiable information is at stake, the act substitutes an administrative process.[32] The law regulates conduct more than information, thereby evading the definitional problem for information that is neither clearly identifiable nor wholly nonidentifiable.

Data Elements and Professional Judgment Standards

In the United States, general federal health privacy standards derive from a rule[33] issued by the Department of Health and Human Services under the authority of the Health Insurance Portability and Accountability Act[34] (HIPAA). The rule defines *individually identifiable health information* to include health information for which there is a reasonable basis to believe that the information can be used to identify an individual.[35] This is an example of a reasonableness standard that by itself provides little interpretative guidance. HIPAA's approach to identifiability does not end with this definition, however. HIPAA offers what may be the most sophisticated approach to identifiability found in any privacy law.

The rule offers two independent methods to turn identifiable (regulated) data into deidentified (unregulated) data. The first method requires removal of 18 specific categories of data elements.[36] With these elements removed, any risk of reidentification is deemed too small to be a concern. The HIPAA rule no longer applies to the stripped data, which can then be used and disclosed free of HIPAA obligations. The only condition is that the covered entity does not have actual knowledge that the information could be used, either on its own or in combination with other data, to identify an individual.[37] The advantage of this so-called safe harbor method is that mechanical application of the rule produces data that can nearly always be treated as wholly nonidentifiable. Some critics claim that the resulting data are useless for many purposes.

The second way to create deidentified (unregulated) health data requires a determination by "a person with appropriate knowledge of and experience with generally accepted statistical and scientific principles and methods for rendering information not individually identifiable."[38] The required determination must be that "the risk is very small that the information could be used, alone or in combination with other reasonably available information, by an anticipated recipient to identify an individual who is a subject of the information."[39] The person making the determination must document the methods used and the results of the analysis on which the determination is based.[40]

HIPAA includes another procedure for disclosure of a limited dataset that does not include overt identifiers but that has more data elements than the safe harbor method. In order to receive a limited dataset, the recipient must agree to a data use agreement that establishes how the data may be used and disclosed, requires appropriate safeguards, and sets other terms for processing.[41] Disclosures under the limited dataset procedure can be made only for activities related to research, public health, and health care operations. A recipient under this procedure is not by virtue of the receipt subject to HIPAA or accountable to the secretary of health and human services, but the agreement might be enforced by the covered entity that disclosed the data or, perhaps, by a data subject.

Litigation

Identifiability issues have arisen in a few court cases.

• One U.S. case involved a commercial dispute between two large health data processing companies. WebMD purchased a company (Envoy) from Quintiles in 2000. As part of the acquisition, WebMD agreed to supply Quintiles with nonidentifiable patient claims data processed by Envoy. Quintiles processes large volumes of data to assess the usage of prescription drugs. Quintiles sells the resulting information in nonidentifiable form primarily to pharmaceutical manufacturers. The litigation arose because of concerns by WebMD that the combination of its data with identifiable data otherwise in the possession of Quintiles would allow reidentification.[42] The resolution of this dispute did not involve a ruling on the identifiability issues raised, but it may be a precursor to other similar battles.

- A United Kingdom case[43] involving identifiability began with a policy document issued by the British Department of Health. The document expressly stated that stripping of identifiers from patient information before disclosure to private data companies seeking information on the habits of physicians is not sufficient to avoid a breach of the physician's duty of confidentiality. Even the disclosure of aggregated data would be a violation of confidentiality. A company that obtains prescription data identifiable to physicians and not patients sued to overturn the policy. The lower court found that disclosure of patient information was a breach of confidence notwithstanding the anonymization. However, an appellate court found the reverse and overturned the department policy. Both courts proceeded on the theory that either personal data were identifiable, or they were not. Neither opinion recognized or discussed any middle ground.

- An Illinois case arose under the state Freedom of Information Act when a newspaper requested information from the Illinois Cancer Registry by type of cancer, zip code, and date of diagnosis.[44] The registry denied the request because another statute prohibits the public disclosure of any group of facts that tends to lead to the identity of any person in the registry. The court reversed and ordered the data disclosed. Although an expert witness was able to identify most of the records involved, the court was not convinced. The court held that the "evidence does not concretely and conclusively demonstrate that a threat exists that other individuals, even those with skills approaching those of Dr. Sweeney, likewise would be able to identify the subjects or what the magnitude of such a threat would be, if it existed." The Illinois Supreme Court upheld the decision in 2006.[45]

- Litigation over the constitutionality of a federal law prohibiting so-called partial birth abortions produced a noteworthy decision on identifiability.[46] The specific dispute was over disclosure during discovery of patient records maintained by physicians testifying as expert witnesses. The records were to be deidentified before disclosure so that a patient's identity could not reasonably be ascertained. The case was decided in part on grounds that there is still a privacy interest even if there were no possibility that the patient's identity could be determined.[47] Arguments that wholly nonidentifiable records retain a privacy interest are unusual, and the conclusion is all the more remarkable because the judge (Richard Posner) is a well-known critic of privacy.

Conclusion

Existing statutes and rules that address deidentification matters can be categorized roughly into three groups. One category establishes standards for determining whether data are sufficiently or potentially identifiable to warrant regulation. The standards can (a) be inward-looking (considering only the data themselves); (b) be outward-looking (considering other data actually or potentially available elsewhere as well as the capabilities for reidentification generally available to individuals or experts); (c) require professional statistical judgment; or (d) consider the time, effort, or cost required for reidentification. This is not an exhaustive list, and multiple standards may apply at the same time.

The second category involves an administrative process. The Alberta law requires an administrative review for privacy of some planned reidentification activities. An administrative process could also review deidentification efforts. Other forms of notice, review, and even approval are possible as well, but the Alberta law is the only known example to date.

The third category is a mechanical rule requiring the removal of specified data elements. While the first two categories are not exclusive—it is possible to have a standard and a process together, for example—a mechanical rule could be a complete alternative for a standard or a process, as HIPAA illustrates.

Statutes, both domestic and international, are all over the lot. The significance of the differences among the various legislative provisions on identifiability is uncertain. It is not clear how much attention legislators paid to identifiability standards, and the statutes may simply offer alternate word formulas produced without much consideration. Better legislative standards on identifiability do not appear to be on anyone's agenda at present.

The few court decisions in the area are no better than the statutes. The abortion records case and the Illinois cancer registry decision reach conclusions that are hard to reconcile. One case found a privacy interest in wholly nonidentifiable data, and the other found no privacy interest in supposedly deidentified records that an expert proved were identifiable. It may be some time before the courts understand the basic issues or produce any meaningful standards on identifiability.

Finally, none of the statutes or court cases expressly addresses location information. Location information is just another data element that may contribute to the identifiability of personal data.

COLLECTION

A second major privacy concern arises with the collection of personal information. In the United States, what personal information may be collected depends on who is doing the collection and what methods are being used. However, much actual and potential personal data collection is unregulated, especially for private parties. For example, many merchants collect transaction and other information from data subjects and from a large industry of data brokers, mailing list purveyors, and other commercial firms. Even the collection of information from web users through spyware was not clearly or expressly illegal anywhere a few years ago, although some spyware may violate unfair and deceptive trade practices laws. In many other countries, however, general standards for collection exist as part of broadly applicable data protection laws, and the collection standards apply generally to all public and private record keepers.

Video Surveillance

Video (and visual) surveillance is of particular interest because it has the capability of recording location in addition to other data elements. Except for surveillance by the government for law enforcement purposes, however, there is little law on video surveillance or the data produced by video surveillance. The lengthy description here is intended to describe standards for personal information collection for arguably public data elements that might apply when statutes are rare or nonexistent.

U.S. laws and policies for all types of surveillance lack clarity, coherence, consistency, compactness, and currency.[48] The rules governing surveillance vary depending on numerous factors. General surveillance jurisprudence in the United States is extensive for criminal matters, and the Fourth Amendment provides important standards for government actions. Surveillance by private parties (other than wiretapping[49]) is only occasionally statutorily regulated, but it maybe actionable through a privacy tort. For all types of visual surveillance, the most important factors are whether it takes place in a public or private place and whether there is a reasonable expectation of privacy. A general rule of thumb (with some exceptions) is that visual surveillance in public space is not restricted.

Supreme Court Decisions

In *Katz v. United States*,[50] the main issue was whether to allow evidence of a telephone conversation overheard by government agents who attached an electronic device to a public telephone booth made of glass. The Supreme Court decided that the surveillance was subject to Fourth

Amendment protection, meaning that the surveillance needed a court order. Importantly, the Court held that the Fourth Amendment protects people and not places. Still, the Court said that "[w]hat a person knowingly exposes to the public, even in his own home or office, is not a subject of Fourth Amendment protection."[51] This statement suggests almost directly that the Fourth Amendment does not protect surveillance in public places. However, the Court did not decide that issue expressly.

In a concurring opinion, Justice John M. Harlan offered a test now widely used to assess when privacy should fall under the protections of the Fourth Amendment. Under the test, a reasonable expectation of privacy exists if (1) a person has exhibited an actual (subjective) expectation of privacy and (2) that expectation is one that society is prepared to recognize as reasonable.[52] When this test is satisfied, a government search or surveillance activity that violates the reasonable expectation of privacy falls under the Fourth Amendment. A well-recognized problem with the reasonable expectation of privacy test is the "silent ability of technology to erode our expectations of privacy."[53]

In *United States v. Knotts*,[54] the government surreptitiously attached an electronic beeper to an item purchased by a suspect and transported in his car. The Court held that "a person traveling in an automobile on public thoroughfares has no reasonable expectation of privacy in his movements from one place to another."[55] *Knotts* implies that virtually any type of visual surveillance in a public place is free of Fourth Amendment constraints. Aware that its decision might be read to allow unrestricted public place surveillance, the Court said that "dragnet-type law enforcement practices" will be considered when they arise.[56]

In *California v. Ciraolo*,[57] police officers in a private airplane flew over a house at an altitude of 1,000 feet and saw marijuana growing in the yard. The issue for the Supreme Court was whether the warrantless aerial observation of a fenced yard adjacent to a home violated the Fourth Amendment. Privacy in a home receives the highest degree of Fourth Amendment protection. However, the Court concluded that observation of the yard from publicly navigable airspace was not unreasonable and that there was no Fourth Amendment protection.

Dow Chemical Company v. United States[58] involved government aerial observation of a large chemical complex with security that barred ground-level public views and limited scrutiny from the air. The Supreme Court held that the complex fell under the doctrine of open fields, so aerial photographs from navigable airspace are not a Fourth Amendment search. The Court suggested (but did not decide) that use of "highly sophisticated surveillance equipment not generally available to the public, such as satellite technology, might be constitutionally proscribed absent a warrant."[59] This decision came in 1986, long before satellite photos were available to every

Internet user. Both this case and the preceding case (*Ciraolo*) were decided by 5 to 4 majorities.[60]

Video Surveillance Statutes Generally

Statutes on video surveillance by private parties are rare but increasing. Recent years have seen a wave of legislation prohibiting video voyeurism. Washington State provides an example. Prior to a 2003 amendment, a statute defined the crime of voyeurism as viewing, photographing, or filming another person without that person's knowledge or consent, while the person is in a place where he or she would have a reasonable expectation of privacy.[61] The law defined a place where an individual would have a reasonable expectation of privacy as being (1) a place where a reasonable person could disrobe in privacy without being concerned about being photographed or (2) a place where a person may reasonably expect to be safe from casual or hostile intrusion or surveillance.[62]

The law had to be changed when the State Supreme Court overturned the conviction of defendants who filmed in public places using a ground-level camera to take photographs up the skirts of women. The so-called upskirt photography took place in public, where there was no expectation of privacy. The state legislature quickly amended the statute, making it a crime to view, photograph, or film the intimate areas of another person without that person's knowledge and consent under circumstances in which the person has a reasonable expectation of privacy, whether in a public or private place.[63] A roughly comparable Arizona law, however, has an exception for use of a child monitoring device,[64] sometimes called a nanny cam.

Other state laws regulate videotaping in particular circumstances. A Connecticut law prohibits employers from operating electronic surveillance devices in employee restrooms, locker rooms, or lounges.[65] Texas passed a so-called granny cam law in 2001 that allows a nursing home resident "to place in the resident's room an electronic monitoring device that is owned and operated by the resident or provided by the resident's guardian."[66] Some laws regulate cameras to catch red light running and cameras for racial profiling oversight.

Privacy Torts

Video surveillance can constitute an invasion of privacy that is actionable through a private lawsuit under state laws, but state laws can vary considerably. Many states have adopted some policies from the *Restatement of Torts (Second)*. The Restatement defines four types of privacy invasions, of which *unreasonable intrusion upon the seclusion of another* is the most important for surveillance purposes.[67] This tort does not depend on any publicity given to the person whose interest is invaded.[68] For the other privacy torts, actionable activities derive from the use to which a name, image, or information is put. Under the intrusion tort, mere surveillance can, under the right circumstances, give rise to a cause of action.

The *Restatement* is clear that the intrusion must occur in a private place or must otherwise invade a private seclusion that an individual has established for his or her person or affairs. The *Restatement* expressly excludes the possibility of liability for taking a photograph while an individual is walking on a public highway. Even in public, however, some matters about an individual "not exhibited to the public gaze" can be actionable. For example, photographing someone's underwear or lack of it could be invasive and actionable as a tort, regardless of a criminal statute.[69]

The public/private distinction so important to Fourth Amendment jurisprudence is equally important to the tort of intrusion upon seclusion. Surveillance of a public place, house, yard, car parked in a public place, at an airport counter, and at similar places would not give rise to liability. Surveillance in a private area, such as a dressing room or bathroom, could create liability.

Tort law recognizes some limits, however. Several precedents find liability for invasion of privacy even though the surveillance took place entirely in public space. Thus, unreasonable or intrusive surveillance of personal injury defendants will give rise to a claim for invasion of privacy. Consumer advocate Ralph Nader successfully sued General Motors for surveilling him and invading his privacy while in public.[70] Jacqueline Kennedy Onassis sued a paparazzo who aggressively followed and photographed her and her children.[71] Finding that the photographer insinuated himself into the very fabric of Mrs. Onassis's life, the court issued a detailed injunction limiting the photographer from approaching her. Extrapolating from the Nader and Onassis cases is difficult, however.

Even regular surveillance of a particular individual may not always support an actionable invasion of privacy. In personal injury cases, for example, it has become common for an insurance company to hire a private investigator to determine the extent of a victim's injuries through surveillance. This type of surveillance is not always invasive, and the courts recognize it as a consequence of filing injury claims.

The use of tort law in response to unreasonable surveillance activities, even in public space, has a firm basis. However, the border between reasonable and unreasonable activities remains uncertain, depending on the facts of each case and the intent of the person conducting the surveillance.

Conclusion

The first issue in assessing the legality of surveillance is whether the surveillance is being done by the government or by a private actor. Rules regulating government surveillance are exquisitely complex, and rules governing private surveillance are mostly nonexistent. For both types of surveillance, however, the two most important factors in distinguishing permissible from impermissible visual surveillance are whether the area being surveilled is public or private and whether there is a reasonable expectation of privacy. However, many questions about the legitimate use of visual surveillance remain unanswered because courts and legislatures often trail technological developments. For the most part, however, there is almost no law that regulates visual surveillance in general or in public places. The implication in *Knotts* that virtually any type of visual surveillance in a public place is free of Fourth Amendment constraints is not an assurance that anything goes for the government, but that may well be the result, at least when an exotic technology is not employed. For private activity, a lawsuit over visual surveillance in public places is always possible, but it might be difficult for a plaintiff to win in the absence of a lewd intent or other showing of bad faith.

The extent to which physical or camera surveillance of an individual is different from the association of location information with an individual is not clear. There is a qualitative difference between being followed or filmed, on one hand, and being tracked electronically with locations recorded (whether continuously or otherwise), on the other.

Whether the association of geocoding with other types of personal data would create any legally recognized violations of privacy is impossible to say. None of the existing precedents is directly on point, and much would depend on facts, intent, methods, locations (public or private), expectations, and uses. Consider the possibility that compiled information would create evidence of a crime, produce a record that would break up a marriage, something that would embarrass a public figure, disclose sensitive medical information (e.g., entering a drug abuse clinic), or constitute grounds for losing a job.

A collection of information that violated an agreement or understanding reached with a research subject might be actionable under several different legal theories, including contract law and tort law. The tort for intrusion upon seclusion is most relevant because it is not dependent on publicity (i.e., use of the information) given to the person whose interest is invaded. The mere collection of information could be enough to sustain a lawsuit. However, proving damages in privacy cases is often challenging, and it could present a significant barrier to recovery in an intrusion. Recovering damages from a researcher would be difficult in many foreseeable factual circumstances. However, ultimate success in litigation might provide limited comfort to a researcher obliged to pay for and live through a lawsuit.

Technology constantly changes the nature of surveillance and blurs the distinctions between traditional categories. Cell phones may (or may not) provide an example of a form of surveillance that is similar to but not quite the same as visual surveillance. Physically following an individual in public space is visual surveillance. Tracking an automobile with a beeper inside on public highways is also visual surveillance. Tracking an individual in public space by means of a cell phone may be different, especially if the phone is not in plain sight. This distinction between visually following an individual and using a cell phone as a tracking device may be important in a criminal context, and the courts are beginning to pay attention.[72] However, criminal jurisprudence is not likely to be of great relevance to researchers.

Commercial tracking of cell phone locations[73] may produce location information, but the availability of tracking information for secondary purposes is unknown and likely to be controlled by service contracts. There do not appear to be any statutes expressly regulating the use of cell phone location information for private purposes. It is common for private repositories of personal information to exist without any statutory regulation. Marketers have voracious appetites for personal data, and they may be a market for using or acquiring location information.

EU Data Protection Directive

Most national privacy laws implement internationally recognized Fair Information Practice principles. The principle for collection limitation states "that there should be limits to the collection of personal data, that data should be collected by lawful and fair means, and that data should be collected, where appropriate, with the knowledge or consent of the subject."[74]

The EU Data Protection Directive[75] implements this policy through several provisions.[76] Article 6(1)(b) requires member states to provide that personal data must be

> collected for specified, explicit and legitimate purposes and not further processed in a way incompatible with those purposes. Further processing of data for historical, statistical or scientific purposes shall not be considered as incompatible provided that Member States provide appropriate safeguards.

This policy is far removed from the anything-goes approach to personal information collection usually found in the United States in the absence of a statute that provides otherwise. In Europe, the purposes for collection and processing must be specific, explicit, and legitimate. That means, among other things, that a data controller must define purposes in advance. Secondary uses may not be incompatible with the stated purposes, and that is a weaker test than an affirmative requirement that secondary uses be compatible.

This provision of the directive provides that processing for historical, statistical, or scientific purposes does not violate the compatibility standard with additional safeguards. That allows disclosures of personal information to researchers and others, but it does not exempt the recipients from complying with data protection standards for the data they are processing.

The directive also requires as a condition of personal data processing (including collection and disclosure) that the data subject has given consent unambiguously. Exceptions to consent include if processing is necessary for the performance of a contract, to comply with a legal obligation, to protect the vital interests of the data subject, to carry out a task in the public interest, or for the purposes of the legitimate interests pursued by the controller.[77] There are more terms and conditions to these exceptions.

European organizations cannot make unrestricted decisions about what to collect. In particular, the last justification for processing—for the purposes of the legitimate interests pursued by the controller—is worthy of additional discussion. It applies except when the data controller's interests are overridden by the interests or fundamental rights and freedoms of the data subject. The specific balance between the use of information for legitimate ordinary business activities (including but not limited to marketing) is something left to member states to decide. The policy allows considerable flexibility in implementation. For example, Great Britain implements the principle by giving individuals a limited right to prevent processing likely to cause damage or distress and an absolute right to prevent processing for purposes of direct marketing.[78] In the United States, by contrast, there is no general right to opt-out of collection, marketing, or other types of processing. Some specific statutes grant limited rights to prevent some uses. Some companies have adopted privacy policies that grant greater rights to data subjects.

One distinction that is important when comparing statutory standards across jurisdictions is the breadth of privacy laws. In countries with omnibus privacy laws, all data controllers are likely to be subject to privacy regulation for identifiable data. Thus, a person who takes deidentified data and reidentifies them is likely to fall under the privacy regulatory scheme generally applicable to all record keepers immediately upon completion of the reidentification. The effect is that a European researcher who may have escaped data protection regulation because of the absence of identifiable data may become subject to regulation by linking that data with additional geographical or other data.

In the United States, however, unless a law directly regulates an entity's information processing activities, it is unlikely that any privacy restrictions will apply. The U.S. health privacy rule known as HIPAA offers an illustration.[79] The rule regulates the use of individually identifiable health information only by covered entities, which are most health care providers and all health plans (insurers) and health care clearinghouses. Others who obtain and use health data and who are not operating as covered entities (or as their business associates) are not affected by the rule in their processing activities. Thus, a researcher, public health department, or court may obtain regulated health data (under specified standards/procedures) without becoming subject to the HIPAA rule.

Selected U.S. Statutes Limiting Collection of Personal Information

Not all existing U.S. privacy statutes limit the collection of personal information. A few examples of collection restrictions illustrate the diversity that exists among the laws.

Privacy Act of 1974

The Privacy Act of 1974,[80] a law that applies only to federal government agencies and to a few government contractors (but no grantees), regulates collection in several ways. First, it allows agencies to maintain only information about an individual as is relevant and necessary to accomplish an agency purpose. Second, it requires agencies to collect information to the greatest extent practicable directly from the data subject if an adverse determination may result. Third, it prohibits the maintenance of information describing how an individual exercises any right guaranteed by the First Amendment, unless authorized by statute or pertinent to an authorized law enforcement activity.[81] For a researcher working for a federal agency who collects and links geographic data, the first two restrictions are not likely to be meaningful, and the third would be relevant only in narrow instances (such as tracking individuals at a political demonstration).

Health Insurance Portability and Accountability Act

The federal health privacy rule, issued by the U.S. Department of Health and Human Services under the authority of the Health Insurance Portability and Accountability Act (HIPAA), reflects generally recognized fair information practices,[82] except that information collection is barely mentioned. The apparent policy is to avoid dictating to health care providers what information they can and cannot collect when treating patients. The only limited exception comes with the application of the HIPAA privacy rule's minimum necessary standard.[83] In general, the rule seeks to limit uses of, disclosures of, and requests for personal health information to the minimum necessary to accomplish the purpose of the use, disclosure, or request. The minimum necessary rule has several exceptions, including a broad one for treatment activities. The rule directs a covered entity requesting personal health information from another covered entity to make reasonable efforts to limit the information requested to the minimum necessary to accomplish the intended purpose of the request. Data collection from a data subject or from any source other than another covered entity is not restricted by the minimum necessary rule.

Children's Online Privacy Protection Act

The Children's Online Privacy Protection Act (COPPA)[84] makes it unlawful for a website operator to collect personal information from a child under the age of 13 without obtaining verifiable parental consent. Personal information includes a physical address. The law appears to apply to website operators located anywhere in the world. The law does not restrict collection of information by phone, fax, or other means or from older children.

Cable Communications Policy Act

Cable television operators may not use their cable system to collect personally identifiable information concerning a subscriber without consent.[85] Exceptions cover service and theft detection activities. The law does not otherwise restrict collection, but it does restrict disclosure.

Conclusion

No general statute regulates personal information collection in the United States. A few U.S. laws restrict the collection of personal information in narrow contexts. The collection of personal information—including information from public sources, from private companies, by direct observation, or by linking of data from disparate sources—is only rarely the subject of overt regulation. Legal challenges to the mere collection of information are likely to be hard to mount in the absence of legislation, but challenges are not impossible. When collected information is used or disclosed, however, different standards are likely to apply than apply to the mere collection of data. Use and disclosure regulations, while still rare, are found more frequently. No known federal law expressly addresses the collection of location information.

DISCLOSURE

A third major privacy concern is the disclosure of personal information. In the United States, disclosure is only sometimes subject to regulation. For many record keepers, the only limits on disclosure come from contracts with data subjects, the possibility of tort lawsuits, or market pressure. Many commercial and other institutions collect and disclose personal information without the knowledge or consent of the data subjects.

Some record keepers are subject to privacy or other laws with disclosure restrictions. Researchers are typically subject to human subject protection rules and to oversight by institutional review boards. In some instances, laws protect narrow classes of research records or statistical data from disclosure. Laws that mandate disclosure—open government or public record laws—may apply to government record keepers and to some others who receive grants from or do business with governments. Examples of all of these laws are discussed below.

Any record may become the subject of a search warrant, court order, subpoena, or other type of compulsory process. Some laws protect records from some types of compulsory process, and these are reviewed here. General laws, rules, and policies about compulsory process will not be examined here, with one exception. A general statute providing for court-ordered disclosures that has received considerable attention is the USA Patriot Act. [86] Section 215 of the act allows the director of the Federal Bureau of Investigation (FBI) to seek a court order requiring the production of "any tangible things (including books, records, papers, documents, and other items) for an investigation to protect against international terrorism or clandestine intelligence activities."[87] The technical procedure is not of immediate interest, but the law requires a judge to issue an order if the request meets the statute's standards. The law also prevents the recipient of an order from disclosing that it provided materials to the FBI. The authority of this section makes virtually every record in the United States accessible to the FBI. It is unclear whether the USA Patriot Act was intended to override laws that protect research records against legal process. There may be different answers under different research protection laws.

The standards for disclosure under the EU Data Protection Directive (a reasonable proxy for most international data protection laws) are mostly the same as the standards described above for collection. The directive generally regulates processing of personal information, and processing includes collection and disclosure. As with collection, a data controller in the EU needs to have authority to make a disclosure (consent, legitimate interest, and others). International standards are not considered further in this section.

Laws Restricting Disclosure by Record Keepers

Most privacy laws restrict the disclosure of personal information by defined record keepers. A brief description of the restrictions from a sample of these laws follows.

Privacy Act of 1974

The Privacy Act of 1974,[88] a law that applies only to federal government agencies and to a few government contractors (but no grantees), regulates disclosure of personal information maintained in a system of records in several ways. Generally, an agency can disclose a record only when the act allows the disclosure or with the consent of the subject of the record. The act describes 12 conditions of disclosure, which generally cover routine disclosures that might be appropriate for any government record (within the agency, for statistical uses, to the U.S. Government Accountability Office, to Congress, for law enforcement, pursuant to court order, etc.). One of the conditions of disclosure is for a routine use, or a disclosure that an agency can essentially establish by regulation.[89] Each system of records can have its own routine uses determined by the agency to be appropriate for the system. As a practical matter, the Privacy Act imposes a clear procedural barrier (publication in the *Federal Register*) to disclosure, but the substantive barriers are low.

Fair Credit Reporting Act

Enacted in 1970, the Fair Credit Reporting Act (FCRA) was the first modern information privacy law. The act tells consumer reporting agencies (credit bureaus) that they can disclose credit reports on individuals only for a permissible purpose. The main allowable purposes are for credit transactions or assessments, employment, insurance, eligibility for a government license, or for a legitimate business need in connection with a transaction initiated by a consumer. Some other governmental, law enforcement, and national security purposes also qualify.[90]

Health Insurance Portability and Accountability Act

The privacy rule issued under the authority of the Health Insurance Portability and Accountability Act controls all disclosures of protected health information by covered entities (health care providers, health plans, and clearinghouses).[91] However, the rule allows numerous disclosures without consent of the data subject. Disclosures for research purposes are permitted if an institutional review board or a privacy board approved waiver of individual authorization.[92] Once disclosed to a researcher, protected health information is no longer subject to regulation under HIPAA (unless the researcher is otherwise a covered entity). However, the researcher will still be subject to the institutional review board that approved the project, which may seek to oversee or enforce the conditions of the disclosure, including restrictions on redisclosure. Whether institutional review boards have adequate oversight or enforcement capabilities is an open question.

Confidential Information Protection and Statistical Efficiency Act

The Confidential Information Protection and Statistical Efficiency Act of 2002 provides generally that data acquired by a federal agency under a pledge of confidentiality and for exclusively statistical purposes must be used by officers, employees, or agents of the agency exclusively for statistical purposes.[93] Information acquired under a pledge of confidentiality for exclusively statistical purposes cannot be disclosed in identifiable form for any use other than an exclusively statistical purpose, except with consent. The law essentially seeks to provide for functional separation of records, which is ensuring that data collected for a research or statistical purpose cannot be used for an administrative purpose.[94] Some other statistical confidentiality laws (see below) offer express protections against subpoenas, but CIPSEA does not directly address legal process. The law's definition of *nonstatistical purpose* can be read to exclude disclosures for legal process, but any exclusion is not express, and the law has not been tested.[95]

Driver's Privacy Protection Act

In 1994, Congress passed a law that prevents the states from disclosing motor vehicle and drivers' license records. As later amended, the Driver's Privacy Protection Act requires affirmative consent before those records can be disclosed.[96] The law allows disclosures for permissible purposes, and one of purposes is for use in research activities and in producing statistical reports.[97] Any personal information so used cannot be published, redisclosed, or used to contact individuals.

Highway Toll Records

At least one state has a strict law protecting the confidentiality of electronic toll collection system (E-Z Pass) records that excludes all secondary uses, apparently including law enforcement and research. New Hampshire law provides that all information received by the department that could serve to identify vehicles, vehicle owners, vehicle occupants, or account holders in any electronic toll collection system in use in this state shall be for the exclusive use of the department for the sole purpose of administering the electronic toll collection system, and shall not be open to any other organization or person, nor be used in any court in any action or proceeding, unless the action or proceeding relates to the imposition of or indemnification for liability pursuant to this subdivision. The department may make such information available to another organization or person in the course of its administrative duties, only on the condition that the organization or person receiving such information is subject to the limitations set forth in this section. For the purposes of this section, administration or administrative duties shall not include marketing, soliciting existing account holders to participate in additional services, taking polls, or engaging in other similar activities for any purpose.[98]

No search was undertaken to locate comparable state laws.

Laws Protecting Research or Statistical Records

Several laws provide stronger protection for research or statistical records, sometimes shielding the records from legal process. These laws vary, sometimes significantly, from agency to agency. It is not clear whether the differences are intentional or are the result of legislative happenstance.

Census Bureau

For records of the Census Bureau, the law prohibits the use, publication, or disclosure of identifiable data (with limited statistical/administrative exceptions). It even provides that a copy of a census submission retained by the data subject is immune from legal process and is not admissible into evidence in court. This may be the most comprehensive statutory protection against judicial use in any law.

Health Agencies

A law applicable to activities undertaken or supported by the Agency for Healthcare Research and Quality protects identifiable information from being used for another purpose without consent and prohibits publication or release without consent.[99] A similar law applies to the National Center for Health Statistics.[100] Neither law expressly addresses protection against legal process, but the U.S. Department of Health and Human Services reportedly believes that both laws can be used to defeat subpoenas.

Justice Agencies

A law protects identifiable research and statistical records of recipients of assistance from the Office of Justice Programs, the National Institute of Justice, and the Bureau of Justice Assistance.[101] The law prohibits secondary uses and makes records immune from legal process or admission into evidence without the consent of the data subject. While the protection appears to be broad, the law yields to uses and disclosures "provided by" federal law. Thus, it appears that any statute or regulation calling for a use or disclosure (including the USA Patriot Act) would be effective.

Controlled Substances Act

Through the Controlled Substances Act, the attorney general can give a grant of confidentiality that authorizes a researcher to withhold identifiers of research subjects.[102] Disclosure of identifiers of research subjects may not be compelled in any federal, state, or local civil, criminal, administrative, legislative, or other proceeding. The scope of protection against compelled disclosure is impressive and more detailed than some other laws.

Institute of Education Sciences

A law applicable to the recently established Institute of Education Sciences at the U.S. Department of Education severely restricts the disclosure of individually identifiable information and includes immunity from legal process.[103] However, this strong protection has a significant limitation added by the USA Patriot Act. That act makes the records available for the investigation and prosecution of terrorism.[104] A court order is required, but the court is obliged to issue the order if the government certifies that there are specific and articulable facts giving reason to believe that the information is relevant to a terrorism investigation or prosecution.

The change in confidentiality protection previously afforded to education records is significant and potentially chilling. First, it illustrates how Congress can easily amend statutory protections afforded to statistical or research records. Second, the change appears to be retroactive, meaning that all records previously obtained under the older, more complete confidentiality regime are no longer protected against terrorism uses. Third, the availability of the records for terrorism eliminates the functional separation previously provided by law.

Public Health Service Act

The Public Health Service Act[105] authorizes the secretary of health and human services to provide a certificate of confidentiality to persons engaged in biomedical, behavioral, clinical, or other research. The certificate protects a researcher from being compelled in any federal, state, or local civil, criminal, administrative, legislative, or other proceedings to identify data subjects.[106] Certificates are not limited to federally supported research. A confidentiality certificate does not protect against voluntary or consensual disclosure by the researcher or the data subject. It is not certain that a certificate protects data if the data subject's participation in the research is otherwise known.

Laws That May Require Disclosure

Open Records Laws

Virtually all government agencies are subject to either federal or state open records laws. The federal Freedom of Information Act[107] permits any person to request any record from a federal agency. The law's personal privacy exemption covers most identifiable information about individuals. The exemption would be likely to protect any personal data contained in research records maintained by government researchers. While many state open records laws are similar to the federal law, some are significantly different. For example, some state open records laws do not provide a privacy exemption at all. In those states, research records might be protected under other exemptions, other state laws, by constitutional limitations, or, conceivably, not at all.

In a 1999 appropriations law, Congress directed the U.S. Office of Management and Budget (OMB) to require federal awarding agencies to ensure that all data produced under a grant be made available to the public through the procedures established under the Freedom of Information Act. The purpose was to provide for the public access to government-funded research data. The extension of the FOIA to government grantees was unprecedented. OMB Circular A-110 contains the implementing rules.[108] The circular defines *research data* to exclude personal information that would be exempt from disclosure under the FOIA's personal privacy exemption "such as information that could be used to identify a particular person in a research study."[109] The possibility for disclosure of identifiable research data is remote, but the OMB standard here—"could be used to identify a particular person"—is not derived expressly from the FOIA itself. It is not clear how the phrase should be interpreted. See the discussion of identifiability standards above.

Public Records

Public records is a term that loosely refers to government records that contain personal information about individuals and that are available for public inspection or copying either in whole or in part.[110] State and local governments, rather than the federal government, maintain most public records. Examples include property ownership records, property tax records, occupational licenses, voting registration records, court records, ethics filings, and many more. Many states disclosed publicly drivers' license data before the federal Driver's Privacy Protection Act restricted such disclosures. [111] Some public records are available only to some users or for some purposes.

Public records are relevant for several reasons. First, they are often source material for commercial or other data activities. Many details of an individual's life, activities, and personal characteristics can be found in public files of government agencies. Regular review of public records may not only reveal current information about individuals but will also permit the compilation of a history of former addresses, roommates, jobs, and other activities. Commercial data companies heavily exploit public records to build personal and household profiles. Second, the records typically contain address information. Third, the continued public availability of public records has become controversial in some states because of privacy and identity theft concerns. Legislatures are reviewing decisions about disclosure of the records.

Conclusion

Some privacy laws include provisions regulating the disclosure of personal information. Other laws regulate the disclosure of narrowly defined categories of records used for statistical or research purposes. Still other laws define the terms under which public records (largely maintained by state and local governments) are publicly available. Open records laws make all government records subject to disclosure procedures, but records containing personal information are often exempt from mandated disclosure. Many records in private hands are unregulated at all for disclosure. There is no overarching theme or policy to be found in the law for disclosure of personal information, and it may require diligent research to determine when or if personal information in public or private hands is subject to disclosure obligations or restrictions.

LIABILITY

Liability for misuse of personal data is a complex issue, and it can be addressed here only briefly. A full treatment would result in a legal treatise of significant length that would not provide significant enlightenment.[112]

Some privacy laws expressly include criminal or civil penalties that may apply to record keepers or to record users. Other laws or policies may apply to specific record keepers. Physicians, for example, have an ethical obligation to protect the confidentiality of patient information, and they could be sued or sanctioned under a variety of laws and theories for breaching that obligation. Credit bureaus are subject to the rules of the Fair Credit Reporting Act, and the law provides for administrative enforcement, civil liability, and criminal penalties.[113] Credit bureaus also have qualified immunity that provides limited protection against lawsuits from data subjects.[114] Some penalties apply to those who misuse credit reports. Most merchants are likely to have neither a statutory nor an ethical obligation to protect client data, but some may have customer agreements or formal privacy policies. Violations of those agreements or policies could give rise to liability under tort or contract law and perhaps under other theories as well.

Officers and employees of statistical agencies are subject to criminal penalties for wrongful disclosure of records.[115] The Confidential Information Protection and Statistical Efficiency Act of 2002 expanded the class of individuals who may be subject to criminal penalties for wrongful disclosure.[116] CIPSEA penalties cover officers and employees of a statistical agency, along with agents. An agent is a broadly defined category that appears to include anyone who a statistical agency allows to perform a statistical activity that involves access to restricted statistical information.[117] An agent must agree in writing to comply with agency rules.

CIPSEA does not include any provision that would expressly authorize a data subject to sue over a wrongful disclosure. However, other laws, including the Privacy Act of 1974, might provide a basis for a lawsuit for an individual against a federal agency that wrongfully used or disclosed personal data. It is unlikely that the courts would conclude that CIPSEA creates a private right of action for an aggrieved data subject against an agency employee or agent who improperly used or disclosed statistical information, but state law might provide a tort or other remedy. The creativity of plaintiff's lawyers in finding a basis for a cause of action for cases with attractive facts should not be discounted. Winning a lawsuit and receiving damages, however, are harder to accomplish.

Because of the patchwork quilt of privacy statutes and legal principles, the administrative, civil, and criminal liability of each record keeper and each record user must be analyzed separately. In the absence of statutes or regulations, the analysis would begin by identifying any duty that a record keeper may have to a data subject. In many instances, there will be no clear duty.

In at least some circumstances, however, it may be possible for a data subject to have a legal remedy against a wholly unrelated third party, regardless of the source of the data used by the third party. The tort for intrusion upon seclusion and the tort for publicity given to private life permit a lawsuit to be filed against another person who has no relationship with the data subject and no defined contractual or statutory duty of confidentiality.[118] The availability of these torts varies from state to state.

An unexplored area of potential liability involves recipients of deidentified data who then reidentify the data subjects. In some instances, exploration of liability begins with a regulation. For example, under the federal health privacy rules issued under the authority of HIPAA, disclosure of a limited data set is permitted for some activities (including research) subject to conditions that include a prohibition against identifying the information. If the recipient is not a covered entity under the rule, then there is no administrative enforcement against the recipient.[119] Other enforcement possibilities may be available regardless of an underlying law.

When a recipient obtains information from an entity that has a confidentiality duty to data subjects, liability over reidentification could arise in several ways. The reidentification activity might violate the agreement under which the data were transferred. The data supplier might be able to sue the recipient for breach of contract. Assuming that any privacy obligation falls directly on the data supplier only and not on the recipient, it is possible that the supplier could be sanctioned administratively for failing to properly control further use of the information.

If a recipient reidentifies data contrary to a contract or a law, it is possible that an aggrieved data subject could sue either the data supplier or the recipient. For the supplier, the principal question would be whether a breach of a duty of confidentiality resulted from an imprudent transfer of deidentified data.

For a lawsuit against the recipient by an aggrieved data subject, the legal preliminaries are more complex. A tort or contract lawsuit may be possible, but a data subject may be unable to sue the recipient relying on the contract because the data subject is not a party to the contract between the data supplier and the recipient. The data subject lacks privity—an adequate legal relationship—to the contract to be able to use the contract to enforce an interest. In general, the requirement for privity can be a major obstacle to enforcement of privacy rights for data subjects.[120]

However, the lack of privity can be trumped in some jurisdictions by the doctrine of third-party beneficiaries. Under current contract law principles, a contract with privacy clauses benefiting a data subject who is not a party to the contract may still be enforceable by the data subject. The conditions are that the parties to the contract (i.e., the supplier and the recipient) intended the data subject to benefit and that enforcement by the data subject is appropriate to achieve the intent of the parties.[121] In other words, a data subject may be able to sue to enforce data protection provisions of a contract despite the lack of privity.[122] The law on third-party beneficiaries varies from jurisdiction to jurisdiction, so different results are possible in different states.

Now consider the class of data recipients that reidentifies data after obtaining the data from public or other sources. These recipients may have no duty to the data subject and no direct relationship or obligation to the data suppliers. For example, Latanya Sweeney demonstrated that U.S. hospital discharge data—publicly available with all overt identifiers removed—can nevertheless be linked to individual patients.[123] In one example, she identified the hospital record of the governor of Massachusetts from records that had been deidentified before public release.[124] A public disclosure of this type of information could support a lawsuit against a researcher, although a public figure might have a more difficult case, especially if a newspaper published the reidentified data. Whether the agency that released the discharge data could also be sued is uncertain.

A federal government agency might conceivably be sued for disclosing potentially identifiable personal information in violation of the Privacy Act of 1974.[125] However, the act also allows agencies to justify disclosures that are compatible with the purpose for which the information was collected. An agency that took steps to allow a disclosure of deidentified data might have a complete defense.[126] In any event, the act may not cover deidentified data at all, and the agency might not be responsible for its subsequent reidentification by another party.

In all of these possible lawsuits, much would depend on the facts. If a reidentified record were used for a research purpose, a data subject might have difficulty convincing a jury that harm resulted. However, if the data were used to deny an insurance policy or to charge a higher price for a mortgage, proof of harm would be enhanced, as would the jury appeal of the case.

Because there are so many institutions, interests, and potential legal standards, no broad conclusion about legal liability for data disclosures can be offered. Some statutes include clear sanctions, but much is uncertain otherwise. A data subject might have a remedy with respect to the disclosure or use of deidentified data that are later reidentified. The type of remedy and the likelihood of success would vary depending on the source of the data, the institutions involved, their relationship with the data subject, and other facts. No known case or statute clearly addresses the possibility of a lawsuit by a data subject over reidentification of personal data.

It is noteworthy, however, that remedies for the misuse and disclosure of identifiable personal information are often weak or absent. It seems unlikely that protections for deidentified data would be easier to achieve through the courts in the absence of clear statutes or other standards. However, the creativity of the plaintiff's bar and the courts should not be discounted should a shocking misuse of data occur.

CONCLUDING OBSERVATIONS

The law surrounding the collection, maintenance, use, and disclosure of personal information by researchers and others is typically vague, incomplete, or entirely absent. The possibility of civil liability to a data subject for collection, use, or disclosure of personal information exists, but lawsuits are not frequent, successes are few, and cases are highly dependent on facts.

However, the research community faces other risks. For example, if an aggressive researcher or tabloid newspaper acquires deidentified research data and reidentifies information about politicians, celebrities, or sports heroes, the story is likely to be front-page news everywhere. The resulting public outcry could result in a major change in data availability or the imposition of direct restrictions on researchers. Many privacy laws originated with horror stories that attracted press attention. When a reporter obtained the video rental records of a U.S. Supreme Court nominee, nervous members of Congress quickly passed a privacy law restricting the use and disclosure of video rental records.[127] The Driver's Privacy Protection Act also had its origins with a horror story.

The demise of Human Resources Development Canada's Longitudinal Labour Force File in the summer of 2000 offers an example of how privacy fears and publicity can affect a research activity. The file was the largest repository of personal information on Canadian citizens, with identifiable information from federal departments and private sources. The database operated with familiar controls for statistical records, including exclusive use for research, evaluation, and policy and program analysis. The public did not know about the database until the federal privacy commissioner raised questions about the "invisible citizen profile."[128] The database was staunchly defended, but the public objections were too strong, and Canada dismantled the database. The case for the database was not helped by its media designation as the "Big Brother Database."[129]

Methods for collecting and using data while protecting privacy interests exist, but how effective they are, how much they compromise research results, and how much they are actually used is unclear. It appears that there is room for improvement using existing policies, methodologies, and practices. However, there may be some natural limits to what can be accomplished. The availability of personal data and the technological capabilities for reidentification seem to increase routinely over time as the result of factors largely beyond control.

Basic transparency rules (for both privacy and human subjects protection) require that respondents be told of the risks and consequences of supplying data. For data collected voluntarily from respondents, it is possible that cooperation will vary inversely with the length of a privacy notice. Even when data activities (research or otherwise) include real privacy protections, people may still see threats regardless of the legal, contractual, or technical measures promised. Reports of security and other privacy breaches are commonplace.

Complex privacy problems will not be solved easily because of the many players and interests involved. Those who need data for legitimate purposes have incentives for reducing the risks that data collection and disclosure entail, but data users are often more focused on obtaining and using data and less on remote possibilities of bad publicity, lawsuits, and legislation. The risk to a data subject is a loss of privacy. The risks to data suppliers and users include legal liability for the misuse of data and the possibility of additional regulation. The risk to researchers, statisticians, and their clients is the loss of data sources. The risk to society is the loss of research that serves important social purposes. These risks should encourage all to work toward better rules governing the use and disclosure of sensitive personal information. Risks can be minimized, but most cannot be eliminated altogether.

Self-restraint and professional discipline may limit actions that threaten the user community, but controls may not be effective against all members of the community and they will not be effective against outsiders. Industry standards may be one useful way to minimize risks, maximize data usefulness, and prevent harsher responses from elsewhere. If standards do not come from elsewhere, however, then the courts and the legislatures may eventually take action. Judicial and legislative actions always follow technological and other developments, and any changes imposed could be harsh and wide-reaching, especially if the issue is raised as a result of a crisis. Privacy legislation often begins with a well-reported horror story.

NOTES

1. *Collection Limitation Principle*: There should be limits to the collection of personal data and any such data should be obtained by lawful and fair means and, where appropriate, with the knowledge or consent of the data subject.
    Data Quality Principle: Personal data should be relevant to the purposes for which they are to be used and, to the extent necessary for those purposes, should be accurate, complete, and kept up-to-date.
    Purpose Specification Principle: The purposes for which personal data are collected should be specified not later than at the time of data collection, and the subsequent use limited to the fulfillment of those purposes or such others as are not incompatible with those purposes, and as are specified on each occasion of change of purpose.
    Use Limitation Principle: Personal data should not be disclosed, made available or otherwise used for purposes other than those specified in accordance with the Purpose Specification Principle except (a) with the consent of the data subject, or (b) by the authority of law.
    Security Safeguards Principle: Personal data should be protected by reasonable security safeguards against such risks as loss or unauthorized access, destruction, use, modification or disclosure of data.

Openness Principle: There should be a general policy of openness about developments, practices and policies with respect to personal data. Means should be readily available of establishing the existence and nature of personal data, and the main purposes of their use, as well as the identity and usual residence of the data controller.

Individual Participation Principle: An individual should have the right (a) to obtain from a data controller, or otherwise, confirmation of whether or not the data controller has data relating to him; (b) to have communicated to him data relating to him within a reasonable time; at a charge, if any, that is not excessive; in a reasonable manner; and in a form that is readily intelligible to him; (c) to be given reasons if a request made under subparagraphs (a) and (b) is denied, and to be able to challenge such denial; and (d) to challenge data relating to him and, if the challenge is successful to have the data erased, rectified, completed, or amended.

Accountability Principle: A data controller should be accountable for complying with measures, which give effect to the principles stated above.

Organisation for Economic Co-Operation and Development (1980).

2. 5 U.S.C. § 552(b)(4).
3. Executive Order 12958.
4. Laws in other countries sometimes extend privacy protections to legal persons. Corporate confidentiality interests (whether arising under privacy laws, through statistical surveys that promise protection against identification, or otherwise) can raise similar issues of identification and reidentification as with individuals. Corporate confidentiality interests are beyond the scope of this paper.

   Another set of related issues is group privacy. Groups can be defined in many ways, but race, ethnicity, and geography are familiar examples. If the disclosure of microdata can be accomplished in a way that protects individual privacy interests, the data may still support conclusions about identifiable racial, ethic, or neighborhood groups that may be troubling to group members. Group privacy has received more attention in health care than in other policy arenas. See Alpert (2000).
5. The term *deidentified* is used here to refer to data without overt identifiers but that may still, even if only theoretically, be reidentified. Data that cannot be reidentified are referred to as wholly nonidentifiable data.
6. See generally Gellman (2001). For more on the growth in information collection and availability, see Sweeney (2001).
7. 15 U.S.C. § 1681 et seq.
8. National Committee on Vital and Health Statistics, Subcommittee on Privacy and Confidentiality (1998a).
9. 5 U.S.C. § 552a.
10. 5 U.S.C. § 552a(a)(4). The value of a fingerprint as an identifier is uncertain. Without access to a database of fingerprints and the ability to match fingerprints, a single fingerprint can rarely be associated with an individual. The same is true for a photograph. For example, a photograph of a four-year-old taken sometime in the last 50 years is not likely to be identifiable to anyone other than a family member.
11. Just to make matters even more complex, the federal Freedom of Information Act (5 U.S.C. § 552) has a standard for privacy that is not the same as the Privacy Act. In *Forest Guardians v. U.S. FEMA* (10th Cir. 2005) available: http://www.kscourts.org/ca10/cases/2005/06/04-2056.htm, the court denied a request for "electronic GIS files . . . for the 27 communities that have a flood hazard designated by FEMA . . . showing all of the geocoded flood insurance policy data (with names and addresses removed) including the location of structures relative to the floodplain and whether the structure insured was constructed before or after the community participated in the NFIP." The court found that disclosure would constitute an unwarranted inva-

sion of privacy, the privacy standard under the FOIA. The court reached this conclusion even though virtually identical information had been released in a paper file. The case turned mostly on the court's conclusion that there was a lack of public interest in disclosure, a relevant standard for FOIA privacy determinations. In striking a balance, the court found that any privacy interest, no matter how small, outweighed no public disclosure interest.

12. Personal information means information that identifies "an individual, including an individual's photograph, social security number, driver identification number, name, address (but not the 5-digit zip code), telephone number, and medical or disability information, but does not include information on vehicular accidents, driving violations, and driver's status." 18 U.S.C. § 2725(3).

13. Personally identifiable information "includes information which identifies a person as having requested or obtained specific video materials or services from a video tape service provider." 18 U.S.C. § 2710 (a)(3).

14. 47 U.S.C. § 551(a)(2)(A).

15. E-Government Act of 2002, Pub. L. 107-347, Dec. 17, 2002, 116 Stat. 2899, 44 U.S.C. § 3501 note §502(4).

16. S.C. 2000, c. 5, § 2(1), available: http://www.privcom.gc.ca/legislation/02_06_01_01_ e.asp.

17. Perrin, Black, Flaherty, and Rankin (2001).

18. Loi No. 78-17 du 6 janvier 1978 at Article 4, available: http://www.bild.net/ dataprFr.htm. A 2004 amendment added these words: "In order to determine whether a person is identifiable, all the means that the data controller or any other person uses or may have access to should be taken into consideration." Act of 6 August 2004 at Article 2, available: http://www.cnil.fr/fileadmin/documents/uk/78-17VA.pdf. The amendment does not appear to have changed the strict concept of identifiability or to have added any reasonableness standard.

19. Joel R. Reidenberg and Paul M. Schwartz, *Data Protection Law and Online Services: Regulatory Responses* (1998) (European Commission), Available: http://ec.europa.eu/ justice_home/fsj/privacy/docs/studies/regul_en.pdf.

20. See Loi No. 78-17 du 6 janvier 1978 (as amended) at Article 32 (IV) (allowing the French data protection authority to approve anonymization schemes), Article 54 (allowing the French data protection authority to approve methodologies for health research that do not allow the direct identification of data subjects), and Article 55 (allowing exceptions to a requirement for coding personal in some medical research activities), available: http://www.cnil.fr/fileadmin/documents/uk/78-17VA.pdf.

21. *Directive on the Protection of Individuals with Regard to the Processing of Personal Data and on the Free Movement of Such Data*, Council Directive 95/46/EC, 1995 O.J. (L 281) 31, at Article 2(a), available: http://europa.eu.int/comm/internal_market/ en/dataprot/law/index.htm.

22. Id. at Recital 26.

23. Council of Europe, *Recommendation No. R (97) 5 of the Committee of Ministers to Member States on the Protection of Medical Data* §1 (1997), available: http://www. cm.coe.int/ta/rec/1997/word/97r5.doc.

24. Council of Europe, *Explanatory Memorandum to Recommendation No. R (97) 5 of the Committee of Ministers to Member States on the Protection of Medical Data* § 36 (1997), available: http://www.cm.coe.int/ta/rec/1997/ExpRec(97)5.htm.

25. Privacy Act 1988 § 6 (2001), available: http://www.privacy.gov.au/publications/ privacy88.pdf.

26. UK Data Protection Act 1998 § 1(1) (1998), available: http://www.legislation.hmso. gov.uk/acts/acts1998/19980029.htm.

27. Canadian Institutes of Health Research, *Recommendations for the Interpretation and Application of the Personal Information Protection and Electronic Documents Act (S.C.2000, c.5) in the Health Research Context* 6 (Nov. 30, 2001), available: http://www.cihr.ca/about_cihr/ethics/recommendations_e.pdf.

1(a) For greater certainty, 'information about an identifiable individual', within the meaning of personal information as defined by the Act, shall include only that information that can:

    (i)   identify, either directly or indirectly, a specific individual; or,
    (ii) be manipulated by a reasonably foreseeable method to identify a specific individual; or
    (iii) be linked with other accessible information by a reasonably foreseeable method to identify a specific individual.

1(b) Notwithstanding subsection 1(a), 'information about an identifiable individual' shall not include:

    (i)   anonymized information which has been permanently stripped of all identifiers or aggregate information which has been grouped and averaged, such that the information has no reasonable potential for any organization to identify a specific individual; or
    (ii) unlinked information that, to the actual knowledge of the disclosing organization, the receiving organization cannot link with other accessible information by any reasonably foreseeable method, to identify a specific individual.

(c) Whether or not a method is reasonably foreseeable under subsections 1(a) and 1(b) shall be assessed with regard to the circumstances prevailing at the time of the proposed collection, use or disclosure.

28. Alberta Health Information Act § 1(p) (1999), available: http://www.qp.gov.ab.ca/Documents/acts/H05.CFM.

29. Id. at § 1(r).

30. Id. at § 1(g).

31. Id. at § 68-72.

32. Nonstatutory administrative reviews of data disclosure may be commonplace. For example, the National Center for Health Statistics in the Department of Health and Human Services uses an administrative review process with a Disclosure Review Board to assess the risk of disclosure for the release of microdata files for statistical research. National Center for Health Statistics, *Staff Manual on Confidentiality* (2004), http://www.cdc.gov/nchs/data/misc/staffmanual2004.pdf.

33. U.S. Department of Health and Human Services, "Standards for Privacy of Individually Identifiable Health Information," 65 *Federal Register* 82462-82829 (Dec. 28, 2000) (codified at 45 C.F.R. Parts 160 & 164).

34. Public Law No. 104-191, 110 Stat. 1936 (1996).

35. 45 C.F.R. § 160.103.

36. Id. at § 164.514(b)(2). The complete list of data elements includes "(A) Names; (B) All geographic subdivisions smaller than a State, including street address, city, county, precinct, zip code, and their equivalent geocodes, except for the initial three digits of a zip code if, according to the current publicly available data from the Bureau of the Census: (1) The geographic unit formed by combining all zip codes with the same three initial digits contains more than 20,000 people; and (2) The initial three digits of a zip code for all such geographic units containing 20,000 or fewer people is changed to 000; (C) All elements of dates (except year) for dates directly related to an individual, including birth date, admission date, discharge date, date of death; and all ages over 89 and all elements of dates (including year) indicative of such age, except that such ages and elements may be aggregated into a single category of age 90 or older; (D) Telephone numbers; (E) Fax numbers; (F) Electronic mail addresses;

(G) Social security numbers; (H) Medical record numbers; (I) Health plan beneficiary numbers; (J) Account numbers; (K) Certificate/license numbers; (L) Vehicle identifiers and serial numbers, including license plate numbers; (M) Device identifiers and serial numbers; (N) Web Universal Resource Locators (URLs); (O) Internet Protocol (IP) address numbers; (P) Biometric identifiers, including finger and voice prints; (Q) Full face photographic images and any comparable images; and (R) Any other unique identifying number, characteristic, or code."

37. Id. at. § 164.514(b)(2)(ii).
38. 45 C.F.R. § 164.512(b)(1).
39. Id. at § 164.512(b)(1)(i). The commentary accompanying the rule includes references to published materials offering guidance on assessing risk, and it recognizes that there will be a need to update the guidance over time. Those materials are Federal Committee on Statistical Methodology, Statistical Policy Working Paper 22, *Report on Statistical Disclosure Limitation Methodology* (1994), available: http://www.fcsm. gov/working-papers/wp22.html; "Checklist on Disclosure Potential of Proposed Data Releases," 65 *Federal Register* 82709 (Dec. 28, 2000), available: http://www.fcsm. gov/docs/checklist_799.doc.
40. 45 C.F.R. § 164.512(b)(1)(ii).
41. 45 C.F.R. § 164.514(e).
42. *Quintiles Transnational Corp. v. WebMD Corp.*, No. 5:01-CV-180-BO(3), (E.D. N.C. Mar. 21, 2002).
43. *R. v. Dept of Health ex parte Source Informatics Ltd.*, 1 All E.R. 786, 796-97 (C.A. 2000), reversing 4 All E.R. 185 (Q.B. 1999).
44. *The Southern Illinoisan v. Illinois Department of Public Health*, 812 N.E.2d 27 (Ill.App. Ct. 2004), available: http://www.state.il.us/court/Opinions/AppellateCourt/ 2004/5thDistrict/June/html/5020836.htm.
45. The Court's opinion focused in significant part on the expert abilities of Sweeney and found a lack of evidence demonstrating whether other individuals could identify individuals in the same fashion. Available: http://www.state.il.us/court/opinions/ SupremeCourt/2006/February/Opinions/Html/98712.htm. The opinion suggests that a different result might be obtained with a better factual showing that identifiability capabilities were more widespread among the population. Just how difficult it would be for others to reidentify the records is not entirely clear. However, both courts ignored the possibility that a recipient of data could hire someone with Sweeney's skills and learn the names of patients. The court's basis for decision does not seem to be sustainable in the long run.
46. *Northwestern Memorial Hospital v. Ashcroft*, 362 F.3d 923 (7th Cir. 2004), available: http://www.ca7.uscourts.gov/tmp/I110H5XZ.pdf.
47. Two quotes from the decision are worth reproducing:

> Some of these women will be afraid that when their redacted records are made a part of the trial record in New York, persons of their acquaintance, or skillful "Googlers," sifting the information contained in the medical records concerning each patient's medical and sex history, will put two and two together, "out" the 45 women, and thereby expose them to threats, humiliation, and obloquy.
>
> * * *
>
> Even if there were no possibility that a patient's identity might be learned from a redacted medical record, there would be an invasion of privacy. Imagine if nude pictures of a woman, uploaded to the Internet without her consent though without identifying her by name, were downloaded in a foreign country by people who will never meet her. She would still feel that

her privacy had been invaded. The revelation of the intimate details contained in the record of a late-term abortion may inflict a similar wound.

48. See generally, Gellman (2005).
49. Extensive rules and laws govern surveillance by wire, whether by government actors or private parties.
50. 389 U.S. 347 (1967).
51. 389 U.S. at 351.
52. 389 U.S. at 361.
53. See Schwartz (1995).
54. 460 U.S. 276 (1983).
55. 460 U.S. at 281.
56. Id. at 284.
57. 476 U.S. 207 (1986).
58. 476 U.S. 227 (1986).
59. Id.
60. In *Kyllo v. United States*, 533 U.S. 27 (2001), the Supreme Court found that police use of heat imaging technology to search the interior of a private home from the outside was a Fourth Amendment search that required a warrant. The case turned in part on the use by the government of "a device that is not in general public use, to explore the details of the home that would previously have been unknowable without physical intrusion." Id. at 40. The broader implications of the Court's standard for technology not in general public use are not entirely clear.
61. Wash. Rev. Code § 9A-44-115.
62. Wash. Rev. Code § 9A-44-115(1)(c).
63. 2003 Wash. Laws § 213 (amending Wash. Rev. Code § 9A-44-115).
64. Ariz. Rev. Stat. § 13-3019(C)(4).
65. Conn. Gen. Stat. § 31-48b(b).
66. Tex. Health & Safety Code § 242.501(a)(5).
67. The other torts are for appropriation of a name or likeness, publicity given to private life, and publicity placing a person in a false light. 3 *Restatement (Second) of Torts* § 652A et seq. (1977)
68. Id. at § 652B.
69. Id. at comment c.
70. *Nader v. General Motors Corp.*, 255 N.E.2d 765 (NY 1970), 1970 N.Y. LEXIS 1618.
71. *Galella v. Onassis*, 487 F.2d 986 (2d Cir. 1973).
72. See, e.g., *In the Matter of an Application of the United States For an Order (1) Authorizing the Use of a Pen Register and a Trap and Trace Device and (2) Authorizing Release of Subscriber Information and/or Cell Site Information*, Magistrate's Docket No. 05-1093 (JO), available: www.eff.org/legal/cases/USA_v_PenRegister/celltracking_denial.pdf_; Brief for amicus Electronic Frontier Foundation at 7, available: http://www.eff.org/legal/cases/USA_v_PenRegister/celltracking_EFFbrief.pdf ("The prospective collection of cell site data will therefore reveal the cell phone's location even when that information could not have been derived from visual surveillance, but only from a physical search" [footnote omitted]).
73. Note, *Harvard Journal of Law and Technology* (fall, 2004).

> Given current database and storage capacities, the door is open for an Orwellian scenario whereby law enforcement agents could monitor not just criminals, but anyone with a cell phone. If it sounds improbable, consider that commercial tracking services already provide real-time location information for families and businesses. (p. 316)

74. Organisation for Economic Co-Operation and Development, *Council Recommenda-tions Concerning Guidelines Governing the Protection of Privacy and Transborder Flows of Personal Data*, 20 I.L.M. 422 (1981), O.E.C.D. Doc. C (80) 58 (Final) (Oct. 1, 1980), available: http://www.oecd.org/document/18/0,2340,en_2649 _34255_1815186_1_1_1_1,00.html .

75. *Council Directive 95/46, art. 28, on the Protection of Individuals with Regard to the Processing of Personal Data and on the Free Movement of Such Data,* 1995 O.J. (L281/47), available: http://europa.eu.int/comm/justice_home/fsj/privacy/law/index_ en.htm.

76. Additional rules govern the processing of special categories of data (racial or ethnic origin, political opinions, religious or philosophical beliefs, trade union membership, and data concerning health or sex life). Generally, explicit consent is necessary for collection of these special categories, with some exceptions.

77. Article 7.

78. UK Data Protection Act 1998 §§ 10, 11 (1998), available: http://www.legislation. hmso.gov.uk/acts/acts1998/19980029.htm.

79. U.S. Department of Health and Human Services, "Standards for Privacy of Individu-ally Identifiable Health Information," 65 *Federal Register* 82462-82829 (Dec. 28, 2000) (codified at 45 C.F.R. Parts 160 & 164).

80. 5 U.S.C. § 552a.

81. Id. at §§ 552a(e)(1), (2), & (7).

82. U.S. Department of Health and Human Services, "Standards for Privacy of Individu-ally Identifiable Health Information," 65 *Federal Register* 82462- 82464 (Dec. 28, 2000).

83. 45 C.F.R. §164.502(b).

84. 15 U.S.C. § 6502.

85. 47 U.S.C. § 551(b).

86. Uniting and Strengthening America by Providing Appropriate Tools Required to Intercept and Obstruct Terrorism (USA Patriot Act) Act of 2001, Public Law No. 107-056, 115 Stat. 272, available: http://frwebgate.access.gpo.gov/cgi-bin/getdoc. cgi?dbname=107_cong_public_laws&docid=f:publ056.107.

87. 50 U.S.C. § 1861.

88. 5 U.S.C. § 552a.

89. The conditions of disclosure are at 5 U.S.C. § 552a(b), with the routine use authority at (b)(2). The definition of *routine use* is at 5 U.S.C. § 552a(a)(7).

90. 15 U.S.C. § 1681b.

91. 45 C.F.R. § 164.512.

92. Id. at § 164.512(i).

93. 44 USC § 3501 note, § 512(a). An exception allows disclosure to a law enforcement agency for the prosecution of submissions of false statistical information under stat-utes imposing civil or criminal penalties. Id. at § 504(g).

94. See Privacy Protection Study Commission, *Personal Privacy in an Information Soci-ety* 573 (1977), available: http://www.epic.org/privacy/ppsc1977report/. See also National Research Council and the Social Science Research Council (1993:34-35).

95. 44 USC § 3501 note, § 502(5).

96. 18 U.S.C. § 2721.

97Id. at § 2721(b)(5).

98. N.H. Rev. Stat. Online § 237:16-e (2004), available: http://www.gencourt.state.nh.us/ rsa/html/XX/237/237-16-e.htm.

99. 42 U.S.C. § 934 (formerly 42 U.S.C. § 299c-3(c)).

100. 42 U.S.C. § 242m(d).

101. 42 U.S.C. § 3789g(a).
102. 21 U.S.C. § 872(c).
103. 20 U.S.C. § 9573. The law formerly applied only to the National Center for Education Statistics.
104. USA Patriot Act of 2001 at § 508 (amending 20 U.S.C. § 9007), Public Law No. 107-056, 115 Stat. 272, available: http://frwebgate.access.gpo.gov/cgi-bin/getdoc.cgi?dbname=107_cong_public_laws&docid=f:publ056.107.
105. 42 U.S.C. § 241(d).
106. The National Institutes of Health encourages investigators working on sensitive biomedical, behavioral, clinical, or other types of research to obtain certificates.
107. 5 U.S.C. § 552.
108. U.S. Office of Management and Budget, Circular A-110 (Uniform Administrative Requirements for Grants and Agreements with Institutions of Higher Education, Hospitals, and Other Non-Profit Organizations) (9/30/99), available: http://www.whitehouse.gov/omb/circulars/a110/a110.html.
109. Id. at .36(d)(2)(i)(A).
110. See generally, Gellman (1995).
111. 18 U.S.C. § 2721.
112. More on this general subject can be found in Perritt (2003).
113. 15 U.S.C. § 1681 et seq.
114. Id. at § 1681s-2.
115. See, e.g., 13 U.S.C. § 214 (Census Bureau employees).
116. 44 U.S.C. § 3501 note § 513. Interestingly, while CIPSEA regulates both use and disclosure of statistical information, id. at § 512, only wrong disclosure is subject to criminal penalties.
117. 44 U.S.C. § 3501 note § 502 ("The term "agent" means an individual—
    (A)(i) who is an employee of a private organization or a researcher affiliated with an institution of higher learning (including a person granted special sworn status by the Bureau of the Census under section 23(c) of title 13, United States Code), and with whom a contract or other agreement is executed, on a temporary basis, by an executive agency to perform exclusively statistical activities under the control and supervision of an officer or employee of that agency;
    (ii) who is working under the authority of a government entity with which a contract or other agreement is executed by an executive agency to perform exclusively statistical activities under the control of an officer or employee of that agency;
    (iii) who is a self-employed researcher, a consultant, a contractor, or an employee of a contractor, and with whom a contract or other agreement is executed by an executive agency to perform a statistical activity under the control of an officer or employee of that agency; or
    (iv) who is a contractor or an employee of a contractor, and who is engaged by the agency to design or maintain the systems for handling or storage of data received under this title; and
    (B) who agrees in writing to comply with all provisions of law that affect information acquired by that agency.")
118. 3 *Restatement (Second) of Torts* §§ 652B, 652D (1977).
119. The HIPAA criminal penalties may not apply, either. See U.S. Department of Justice, Office of Legal Counsel, *Scope of Criminal Enforcement Under 42 U.S.C. § 1320d-6* (June 1, 2005), available: http://www.usdoj.gov/olc/hipaa_final.htm.
120. See, e.g., Reidenberg (1992).
121. *Restatement (Second) of Contracts* §§ 302, 303 (1981).

122. The original draft HIPAA privacy rule required business partner agreements to state that the agreements intended to create third-party beneficiary rights. In the final rule, the third-party beneficiary language was removed. The commentary stated that the rule's intent was to leave the law in this area where it was. The discussion in the final rule shows that there were strongly divergent views on the issue. See 65 *Federal Register* 82641 (Dec. 28, 2000).

123. Considerable amounts of patient-level information are available. For example, the Healthcare Cost and Utilization Project distributes four databases for health services research, with data dating back to 1988. This joint federal-state partnership is sponsored by the Agency for Healthcare Research and Quality, a part of the federal Department of Health and Human Services. The databases contain patient-level information for either inpatient or ambulatory surgery stays in a uniform format "while protecting patient privacy." Healthcare Cost and Utilization Project, *Description of Healthcare Cost and Utilization Project* (undated), available: http://www.ahcpr.gov/downloads/pub/hcup/appkitv15b.pdf. Whether the privacy protections are adequate to protect against reidentification under all conditions is uncertain. Numerous other medical data sets are available from other sources.

124. See National Committee on Vital and Health Statistics, Subcommittee on Privacy and Confidentiality (1998b).

125. 5 U.S.C. § 552a.

126. 5 U.S.C. § 552a(b)(3) allows agencies to define a routine use to justify a disclosure.

127. Video Privacy Protection Act ("Bork Law"), 18 U.S.C. § 2710.

128. Privacy Commissioner (Canada), *Annual Report 1999-2000* available: http://www.privcom.gc.ca/information/ar/02_04_09_e.asp.

129. McCarthy (2000).

REFERENCES

Alpert, S.
  2000 Privacy and the analysis of stored tissues. Pp. A-1–A-36 in *Research Involving Human Biological Materials: Ethical Issues and Policy Guidance* (Volume II Commissioned Papers). Rockville, MD: National Bioethics Advisory Commission. Available: http://bioethics.georgetown.edu/nbac/hbmII.pdf. [accessed December 2006].

Gellman, R.
  1995 Public records: Access, privacy, and public policy. *Government Information Quarterly* 12:391-426.
  2001 *Public Record Usage in the United States.* Paper presented at the 23rd International Conference of Data Protection Commissioners, September 25, Paris, France. Available: http://www.personaldataconference.com/eng/contribution/gellman_contrib.html [accessed December 2006].
  2005 A general survey of video surveillance law in the United States. In S. Nouwt, B.R. de Vries, and C. Prins, eds., *Reasonable Expectations of Privacy? Eleven Country Reports on Camera Surveillance and Workplace Privacy.* Hague, Netherlands: T.M.C. Asser Press.

Harvard Journal of Law and Technology
  2004 Who knows where you've been? Privacy concerns regarding the use of cellular phones as personal locators. *Harvard Journal of Law and Technology* 18(1):307, 316 (fall).

McCarthy, S.
    2000   Ottawa pulls plug on big brother database, Canadians promised safeguards on
           data. *Globe and Mail*, May 30.
National Committee on Vital and Health Statistics, Subcommittee on Privacy and Confidentiality
    1998a *Proceedings of Roundtable Discussion: Identifiability of Data*. Hubert Humphrey
           Building, January 28, Washington, DC. Transcript available:
           http://ncvhs.hhs.gov/980128tr.htm [accessed December 2006].
    1998b *Roundtable Discussion: Identifiability of Data*. Available: http://ncvhs.hhs.gov/
           980128tr.htm [accessed January 2007].
National Research Council and the Social Science Research Council
    1993   *Private Lives and Public Policies*. G.T. Duncan, T.B. Jabine, and V.A.. de Wolf,
           eds. Panel on Confidentiality and Data Access. Committee on National Statis-
           tics, Commission on Behavioral and Social Sciences and Education.Washington,
           DC: National Academy Press.
Organisation for Economic Co-Operation and Development
    1980   *Council Recommendations Concerning Guidelines Governing the Protection of
           Privacy and Transborder Flows of Personal Data*. O.E.C.D. Doc. C (80) 58
           (Final). Available: http://www.oecd.org/document/18/0,2340,en_2649_34255_
           1815186_1_1_1,00.html [accessed December 2006].
Perrin, S., H.H. Black, D.H. Flaherty, and T.M. Rankin
    2001   *The Personal Information Protection and Electronic Documents Act: An Anno-
           tated Guide*. Toronto, Canada: Irwin Law.
Perritt, H.H., Jr.
    2003   *Protecting Confidentiality of Research Data through Law*. Paper prepared for
           Committee on National Statistics, National Research Council Data Confidenti-
           ality and Access Workshop, Washington, DC. Available: http://www7.national
           academies.org/cnstat/Perritt_Paper.pdf [accessed January 2007].
Reidenberg, J.R.
    1992   The privacy obstacle course: Hurdling barriers to transnational financial ser-
           vices. *Fordham Law Review* 60:S137, S175.
Reidenberg, J.R., and P.M. Schwartz
    1998   *Data Protection Law and Online Services: Regulatory Responses*
           Commissioned from ARETE by Directorate General XV of the Commission of
           the European Communities. Available: http://ec.europa.eu/justice_home/fsj/pri-
           vacy/docs/studies/regul_en.pdf [accessed December 2006].
Schwartz, P.
    1995   Privacy and participation: Personal information and public sector regulation in
           the United States. *Iowa Law Review* 80:553, 573.
Sweeney, L.
    2001   Information explosion. Chapter 3 in P. Doyle, J. Lane, J. Theeuwes, and L.
           Zayatz, eds., *Confidentiality, Disclosure, and Data Access: Theory and Practical
           Applications for Statistical Agencies*. New York: North-Holland Elsevier.

Apppendix B

Ethical Issues Related to Linked Social-Spatial Data

Felice J. Levine and Joan E. Sieber

The ethics of research related to linking geographically explicit spatial data[1] and individual-, household-, or group-level social data is an issue of scientific and social significance. The capacity to measure location and context over time and with exact precision offers substantial opportunities to comprehend human, social, biological, and environment activities, interactions, and transformations at a level of sophistication that could not have been anticipated just a decade ago. The mesh of technological advances, computational capacity, multilevel statistical models, spatial analysis software, and robust data mining and management techniques makes it a ripe time for new explorations and applications to come to the fore using very precise locational information.[2] Along with these improved measurements and analytic methods come ethical issues regarding how best to use these new capabilities consonant with protecting the interests of research participants involved in such studies.

The most immediate ethical issue raised by linking different datasets or resources of any form is whether the integration of such information encroaches on the privacy of research subjects or compromises the confidentiality of information that otherwise is secure. Attention to issues of privacy of persons and confidentiality of data has increased over recent years.[3] There is growing awareness of the scientific value of sharing data, the greater contributions made possible with microlevel data, and the potential uses from linking different datasets. Yet there is also mindfulness of the potential risks of confidentiality breaches due to intentional or inadvertent disclosure. In this current context, not unexpectedly, opportunities for linking social and spatial data have also been accompanied by serious discussion of the confidentiality issues and policies involved in doing so (see, e.g., Rindfuss and Stern, 1998; VanWey et al., 2005; Golden, Downs, and Davis-Packard, 2005; Gutmann et al., 2005).

Whether in the biomedical or the social-behavioral sciences, new methodological capabilities or work at the frontiers of discovery invariably requires fresh consideration of ethical issues as an integral part of research. Especially in nascent areas of science in which practical experience is limited, grappling with ethical issues needs to go hand-in-hand with confronting theoretical, methodological, and operational considerations.[4] Thus, it is notable that those attracted to or engaged in linking spatial and social data have already initiated the process of thinking reflectively and constructively about matters of confidentiality and reduction of the risk of information disclosure. The establishment of a National Research Council Panel on Confidentiality Issues Arising from the Integration of Remotely Sensed and Self-Identifying Data, with funding from the National Institutes of Health, the National Science Foundation, and the National Aeronautics and Space Administration, to address such confidentiality issues is a strong indicator of the salience of this topic to data producers, users, archivists, database managers, and those who review and support such work.

The purpose of this paper is to consider the ethical issues that come into play in research that links social and spatial data. Our aim is to present an overview of the ethical issues regarding the protection of human subjects, for researchers engaged in primary collection of social and spatial data, and for those engaged in secondary use of such data. First, we briefly highlight the ethical guidance available for researchers or research teams as they consider how best to undertake research on these data or provide such data to others. Second, we elaborate on and recommend as guidance the framework of ethical principles enunciated in the now classic 1979 Belmont Report, *Ethical Principles and Guidelines for the Protection of Human Subjects of Research* (National Commission for the Protection of Human Subjects of Biomedical and Behavioral Research, 1979). Third, we consider the range of ways ethical issues can manifest themselves in the course of collecting, providing, or using linked social-spatial data and how researchers might best advance ethically sound research and approach review by an institutional review board (IRB). Fourth, we examine such issues as consent, privacy and confidentiality, benefits and harm, and assessments of risk of harm and how to address them in research that either links or uses linked social-spatial data. Fifth, we specifically discuss the ethics of data dissemination, sharing, and access—emphasizing issues important to social-spatial research. Finally, we consider ethics education and training for those who collect, prepare, provide access to, use, or review research that links social and spatial data.

This focus on ethical considerations in social and spatial research is distinct from an analysis of the legal requirements that could apply depending on the data that are to be obtained. Use of extant information sources may be protected by privacy laws. Some of the most promising social and spatial research is addressed to issues in which privacy regulations are germane. Health research, for example, is a key area of inquiry in which access to confidential records, including precise locational information, could have tremendous scientific value and benefits to society. The Health Insurance Portability and Accountability Act of 1996 (HIPAA)[5] protects individual privacy but allows for the use of health records for research without individual authorization. Such research needs to be evaluated as no more than minimal risk and needs to conform with a set of procedures and alternative methods to avert disclosure (e.g., meeting 18 specified criteria for deidentification, having a qualified expert determine what needs to be done to prepare the data for release).[6] While researchers, data providers, and research analysts need to be mindful of legal requirements in planning their research, our purpose is directed to the ethical considerations that should guide collecting, gaining access to, analyzing, disseminating, or sharing such data irrespective of whether certain standards of privacy and confidentiality are required by law.

In emphasizing ethical considerations in research linking social and spatial data, we also do not intend to sidestep attention to the human research protection programs in place at academic or research institutions or the centrality of their IRBs for approval and oversight of research. Nor do we intend to minimize the challenge that can be involved in raising complex ethical issues to IRBs in areas in which the decision-making procedures are not yet developed. We do discuss the IRB review process directly. Our purpose in taking a broader approach to ethical decision making with social and spatial data is to focus attention on the research enterprise itself and how best to weigh factors in planning and executing research or in using or making accessible linked social-spatial data. We consider interaction with IRBs to be a key step in that process. While IRBs have direct institutional responsibility for the review of protocols and determinations about human research protection as stipulated in the Code of Federal Regulations for the Protection of Human Subjects (45 CFR 46),[7] we see this interaction between researcher (producer/user) and IRB, and how to navigate it, as a part of the process of ethical decision making in human research, not as constituting that process in and of itself. Furthermore, many decisions having ethical implications are identifiable to the researcher not only prior to interacting with the IRB but also afterward; we regard these latter decision points to be integral to the overall process of ethical conduct.

ETHICAL GUIDANCE AND HUMAN RESEARCH PROTECTION

Given the social and behavioral science backgrounds of many of those engaged in social and spatial research, it might be expected that ethical norms would primarily derive from frameworks in these and adjacent fields. Although there are variations among codes of conduct (e.g., whether or not a code of ethics explicitly encourages data sharing), general standards in the social sciences have much in common regarding such issues as informed consent, intrusions on privacy, confidentiality and its limits, and benefits and harm. Whether the codes were promulgated in detail by the American Psychological Association (2003) or the American Sociological Association (1997) or in more summary fashion by the American Anthropological Association (1998), the Association of American Geographers (1998), the American Political Science Association (1998), the American Statistical Association (1999), or the American Association for Public Opinion Research (2003), there is on balance considerable consistency in their guidance.

One visible marker of specific interest in ethical considerations related to spatial data is the approval in 2003 of a geographic information systems (GIS) code of ethics by the Urban and Regional Information Systems Association (2003). By design, the code builds on a study of several dozen other codes. It states, among other guidance, that the GIS professional will protect individual privacy, especially about sensitive information; will encourage individual autonomy, including allowing individuals to withhold consent from being in a database, correct information, or remove themselves from a database; and will avoid undue intrusions into the lives of individuals (Urban and Regional Information Systems Association, 2003).

Exposure to research with human participants and related codes of conduct is by no means uniform among scientists and other specialists engaged in social and spatial research. Experts in remote sensing and other sophisticated locational measurements are typically not from the social and behavioral sciences or the health sciences, in which individuals or groups are the focus of inquiry and in which ethical guidance emphasizes the protection of human participants in research. Thus, in addition to the scientific richness of this interdisciplinary arena of study, there is also the challenge of fostering a deep appreciation among diverse researchers and research communities of the ethical issues at stake at each stage of the research process, from primary data collection through secondary use.

A second challenge flows from the fact that there is very limited research-based evidence about how ethical issues related to human research protection play out in the context of the collection or use of social and spatial research. In general, empirical study of ethical issues is far too scant across even well-established domains of inquiry, let alone new areas of research.[8] The small body of literature addressed to linking social and spatial data evidences an appreciation that this research area is a dynamic and fluid one and that expert knowledge can help produce research approaches that maximize advancing science consonant with human research protection principles. For example, Armstrong, Rushton, and Zimmerman (1999) do so by examining alternative methods of masking individual-level health data, testing the security of each approach for preserving confidentiality while permitting important uses. Similarly, Kwan, Casas, and Schmitz (2004) test three geographic masks with different perturbation radii to identify the optimum tradeoff between data confidentiality and accuracy of analytic results. These forms of empirical examination hold promise of producing useful guidance. Less directly, but also germane, Kwan and Lee (2004), using three-dimensional geovisualization methods and activity–travel diary data, found gender differences in time use, mobility, and travel patterns, but at the same time they cautioned that "individual-level activity–travel data geocoded to street addresses, given their reasonable degree of positional accuracy, may lead to considerable risk of privacy violation" (p. 63).[9]

THE BELMONT PRINCIPLES AS AN ETHICAL FRAMEWORK

In addition to drawing on ethics codes, recent national commissions, and relevant National Research Council panels, contemporary discussions of ethical considerations with social and spatial data (largely directed to issues of confidentiality) are taking place in the context of more than a 30-year history of ongoing attention to these issues in research and writing.[10] More visible than any other, the Belmont Report articulated three overarching ethical principles that continue to offer a framework for responsible research conduct as well as form the basis of the Code of Federal Regulations for the Protection of Human Subjects (45 CFR 46). This report, issued by the National Commission for the Protection of Human Subjects of Biomedical and Behavioral Research, states the purpose of these principles as follows (p. 3):

Three principles, or general prescriptive judgments, that are relevant to research involving human subjects are identified in this statement.

> Other principles may also be relevant. These three are comprehensive, however, and are stated at a level of generalization that should assist scientists, subjects, reviewers and interested citizens to understand the ethical issues inherent in research involving human subjects. These principles cannot always be applied so as to resolve beyond dispute particular ethical problems. The objective is to provide an analytical framework that will guide the resolution of ethical problems arising from research involving human subjects.

Thus, in setting forth these principles, the commission sought not to dictate but to create a culture of ethical decision making that could effectively serve researchers and IRBs alike.

The three ethical principles that are the foundation of the Belmont Report are respect for persons, beneficence, and justice. Depending on the complexities of a situation, the Belmont Report emphasizes that ethical decision making can—and often does—require balancing competing claims in order to accomplish the overall goals of the principles themselves. Briefly put, the principles are defined as:

1. Respect for Persons—Respect for persons incorporates at least two ethical convictions: first, that individuals should be treated as autonomous agents, and second, that persons with diminished autonomy are entitled to protection. . . . In most cases of research involving human subjects, respect for persons demands that subjects enter into the research voluntarily and with adequate information. . . .

2. Beneficence—Persons are treated in an ethical manner not only by respecting their decisions and protecting them from harm, but also by making efforts to secure their well-being. . . . The obligations of beneficence affect both individual investigators and society at large, because they extend both to particular research projects and to the entire enterprise of research. . . .

3. Justice—Who ought to receive the benefits of research and bear its burdens? This is a question of justice, in the sense of "fairness in distribution" or "what is deserved." An injustice occurs when some benefit to which a person is entitled is denied without good reason or when some burden is imposed unduly. . . .

It is the application of the principles of the Belmont Report that leads to considerations of informed consent, risk-benefit assessment, and the selection of subjects for research. As specified in the Belmont Report, respect for persons requires *informed consent* of research participants—meaning the provision of adequate information, participants' comprehension of that information, and their voluntariness to be part of the research. *Assessment of risk and benefits* of research is closely related to beneficence—including an assessment of the probability of experiencing a harm, the magnitude of that harm (whether physical, psychological, legal, social, or economic), and the benefits that might derive to research participants or society from that research. The importance of risk reduction is also a concept emphasized in the Belmont ethical guidance. The third Belmont principle—justice—is embodied in the requirement that the *selection of subjects* needs to be appropriate to the research and ought not to place an undue burden on certain populations or disadvantage them through omission as research participants.[11]

Privacy and confidentiality are not explicitly mentioned in the Belmont Report, although they follow from the principles of respect for persons and beneficence and both are made explicit in 45 CFR 46.[12] *Privacy* refers to the interest that persons have in controlling others' access to them and private information about them. Individuals can vary in what they consider intrusive about themselves. In a research context, as long as human subjects willingly agree to participate in the research, can freely decide against providing certain forms of information, and can end their participation at any point, they have preserved their privacy right to control their information.

Confidentiality refers to how data will be handled by researchers, other data producers, and ultimately secondary analysts consonant with agreements with human subjects regarding private information.[13] A corollary to participants' providing access to information in this trusting relationship is that researchers have the ethical responsibility to avoid intrusion on participants' privacy and to minimize the likelihood of harm from the disclosure of private information (both identity and attribute disclosure[14]). This commitment takes the form of a *confidentiality agreement* that provides assurances to research participants about what will be done with identifiable and private information about them. Except when data are collected *anonymously* (i.e., without identifying information) or the researcher is collecting only public information, the Belmont principles of respect for persons and beneficence lead researchers to consider confidentiality as part of the consent process and put into place data protection plans to reduce the likelihood of *personal identification*.

Like privacy and confidentiality, ethical guidance on *data sharing* can be deduced from the Belmont Report, but data sharing is not explicitly addressed in either this document or in 45 CFR 46. Much of ethical guidance in human research has focused on the intervention, interaction, and information acquisition processes. There has been far less attention to dissemination of results, access to data, or subsequent data use.[15] The Belmont principle of beneficence emphasizes the value of addressing benefits that can accrue to participants, similarly situated others, and the larger society as well as to the entire research enterprise. Broad in its scope, this principle is particularly applicable to weighing gains that can come from data sharing—including the verification of results, consideration of competing hypotheses, and examination of new questions.

Overall the Belmont principles and derivative applications provide desiderata to help inform the ethical conduct of social and spatial research. Since the Belmont principles were developed primarily by physicians, they do reflect a conception of harm and benefit more appropriate to biomedical research than to social and behavioral science research. This emphasis is problematic when the primary ethical concern is a possible invasion of privacy or a confidentiality breach due to using analytically precise coordinate data rather than when the concern is direct risk of physical harm. Similarly, the notion of autonomy set forth in the Belmont principles and operationalized via informed consent is much harder to understand when the choice is whether to participate in a survey linked to a complex set of locational measurements rather than when the choice is whether to participate in a treatment program that involves specific physical risks and benefits to the individual. Nevertheless, although the Belmont principles leave room for debate and uncertainty when applied to social and behavioral phenomena, the basic concerns of the principles and their emphasis on nuanced ethical decision making commend their use.

By design, the principles offer not answers, but expectations for balancing important considerations in undertaking ethically responsible research. The Belmont principles undergird the Federal Regulations for the Protection of Human Subjects and are also pervasively used across fields of human research. Their strength, however, lies in comprehending the flexibility that they were intended to foster, not in invoking them in a formulaic fashion. No ethical principles taken off the shelf can resolve dilemmas. Thus, in using the Belmont principles, researchers, data providers, and secondary analysts need to extrapolate from them to think through how they apply to social and spatial research.

ETHICAL CONSIDERATIONS, THE RESEARCH CONTEXT, AND RESEARCH PLANNING IN SOCIAL AND SPATIAL RESEARCH

Ethical Considerations

In general, the collection, use, and analysis of linked social-spatial data raise ethical issues that parallel those involved generally in handling identifiable, large-scale data sets on individuals or groups, whether the data are acquired directly or indirectly, and specifically when research involves linkages among microlevel data. Although not as powerful an individual identifier as DNA or other genetic material used in genetic studies, precise coordinate data in the social sciences is at once an identifier and a compelling social indicator that rivals most other forms of contextual measurement because it is location-specific and can be collected repeatedly, in multiple sites, and on a very large scale. It is rare, perhaps even unique, to have a single measure or indicator essentially serve as an exact identifier, either alone or in combination with only a few other variables.

The ethical principles and applications enunciated in the Belmont Report provide a framework for unraveling some of the complexities of social-spatial research. The ethical issues are at one level familiar ones: grappling

with how best to honor confidentiality agreements with research participants, minimize risk of disclosure of private information and potential
harm, and maximize the benefits that can flow from research and access to
the data. The potential identifiability of individuals and groups in studies
involving linked social-spatial data makes it important for researchers to
consider informed consent and the situations in which it can be waived; the
nature of confidentiality agreements and protections; the risk of breaches of
confidentiality and steps to ameliorate that risk; the magnitude of any
potential harm from disclosure; and the benefits that can accrue to participants, their communities, or the larger society.

Attending to these considerations does not per se distinguish social and
spatial research from other inquiries that cannot be undertaken anonymously or that involve identifiable and potentially sensitive personal information. With precise spatial data, the threshold for identifiability may be
lower than in research in which analytic measures are not also personal
identifiers, but the ethical principles shaping researchers' responsibilities
are the same. Technological advances that can aid research can also contribute to increasing the probability of identification. For example, research
using video recordings to study behavior in public places or that have
research participants use wearable computers to monitor movement and
interactions in work or social groups has considerable scientific potential,
but it can also increase the risk of identifiability, even if the consequent
harm is quite minimal. Similarly, spatial measurements are sufficiently precise in that they are at once invaluable to research and yet could make
difficult protecting the identities of individuals and information about them
from inadvertent or intrusive disclosure.

The very complexity of undertaking research of this genre does not
mean that the work inherently involves more than minimal risk in terms of
the type of harm or the likelihood of its occurrence. Also, research procedures can be put into place to reduce or ameliorate risk to a minimal level.
Responsible conduct in research commends the use of advanced measurements and technologies to maximize scientific progress and the benefits of
research while ensuring that any risk of harm for participants remains low.

Contexts of Research

In research involving the linkage of social and spatial data, there are a
large number of persons who collect, use, or otherwise make decisions
about how to maintain, preserve, and make such information available.
Depending on the context, different individuals connected with the research
may take on various roles in the development of a particular human research protection plan or the articulation of a strategy that will engender
confidence in data sharing and use. The basic principles underlying ethical

decision making, whether by data producers or users, are no different from those in similarly complex, large-scale studies about people and their lives in which there can be data from multiple sites, multiple sources, and multiple time points. In all such research, there is an interest in and commitment to enhancing access and use in order to maximize addressing important issues while ensuring that confidentiality agreements are honored and the risk of personal identification is minimal.

Linkages between spatial and social data are being made by researchers at every point in the research enterprise, from primary to secondary use. For example, investigators are specifying designs that incorporate precise coordinate data in the research (e.g., home, workplace, school, recreation center; more than one location) or link to extant databases that provide precise coordinates. Secondary analysts, too, are examining individual-, household-, or group-level behaviors by using data that have those links or by enhancing those data through integrating additional resources. Even in the absence of precise spatial data, the merger of two deidentified databases or one set of public records and one or two deidentified databases raises the possibility of the reidentification of research participants. Identification is even more likely when highly refined locational data are in the mix and are intended to be used as analytic variables.

The data producer and user face particularly challenging circumstances when they generate new data or pursue data integration, analysis, dissemination of results, and sharing or transferring of these data to others. The archivist and the database manager also have responsibilities for how such data are to be preserved, stored, and potentially used.[16] Finally the secondary analyst has the ethical responsibility to honor agreements for access, which include those agreements made with research participants as to use.

Purposive Planning

From the vantage of human research protection and review of research by an institutional review board, there are some immediate ethical questions for primary researchers and secondary users to consider. It is optimal, for example, to determine in advance whether data collection or linked analyses will be individually identifiable only by virtue of obtaining and using locational data; whether or not the consent of research participants will be obtained and, if so, in what form and with what assurances; and whether the likely benefits and the potential harms can be specified, and, in the case of potential harms, whether steps can be taken to ensure that they are low (e.g., embarrassment versus legal liability) and the risks of their occurrence are minimal (through strong data protection or access plans). A primary data producer and user can consider most of these issues in advance of initiating research or can specify them for follow-up review, up to and including strategies for data dissemination and sharing.

The secondary analyst does not create the data or the conditions for the research; nevertheless, she or he needs to develop a research plan consonant with confidentiality protections and needs to seek IRB review to the extent that the new work contemplates the integration of heretofore unlinked datasets or spatial measures.[17] In the case of secondary data, the data archivist, data collector, or initial researcher can require licensing or other contractual arrangements with the secondary user or her or his institution, or the secondary user may need to work in a data enclave or other restricted-access environment in order to use the data. Each of these steps adds a level of review as a condition of access, controls the nature of that access, and includes the force of law to enhance confidentiality protections (see National Research Council, 2000, 2005).[18] The extent to which such steps are necessary or appropriate depends on whether there is more than a minimal risk of disclosure and the probability of harm that any disclosure could entail.

Ethically responsible conduct in the collection or use of social and spatial data is sufficiently complex that it requires a planned, deliberative process. One useful way to think about the preparation of a protocol for review by an IRB, as well as the review process itself, is as a structured opportunity for primary researchers or secondary analysts to present to a group of peer scientists and community members a human research protection plan and approaches for undertaking sound and ethically responsible work. Because of the challenging issues involved in human research protection with social and spatial data, there are core ethical questions that need to be addressed: Is this human subjects research? Does the use of precise coordinate data add value to the topic under study? What is the process for gaining consent or the rationale underlying a request for a waiver of consent? How are issues of confidentiality to be addressed? What are the benefits of the research, and what are the risks of harm and strategies for amelioration? Each of these issues is considered in the next section.

THE BELMONT PRINCIPLES AND QUESTIONS TO GUIDE ETHICAL DECISION MAKING

The principles and standards specified in the Belmont Report provide a useful tool for the responsible planning and implementing of social and spatial research. For example, they can guide in assessing whether exact spatial data affect determinations of what constitutes human subjects research; judging the risks and benefits of certain research topics; and sorting out issues of confidentiality, data access, and data sharing. Fundamental to weighing how research can be done, how research data can be secured, and how access to data can be provided are considerations of respect for the autonomy of human subjects, appreciation of their voluntariness, and assessment of the benefits for subjects and the research enterprise while assessing the risk of harm, the justness of inquiries, and the equitable distribution of benefits and burdens. These ethical principles help to frame questions that inform responsible decision making.

Human Subjects Research

Social and spatial research that otherwise involves no interaction or intervention can become human subjects research as defined in the Federal Regulations for the Protection of Human Subjects because precise coordinate data allows for *personal identification*. The Belmont principles are directed to the conduct of research *with* human subjects, and these principles shape the boundaries of what constitutes human subjects research in the federal regulations. There is considerable research in the social sciences using public records or other information that is publicly available or observable that is not human subjects research, even though it meets the research standard of contributing to generalizable knowledge.[19] Information gathered without intervention or interaction with individuals or without *identifiable private information*[20] is considered to be outside the scope of human subjects research. Also, identifiable information about individuals that is publicly available is not identifiable *private* information, and hence it is also outside the scope of human subjects research.

Highly refined coordinate data can shift otherwise public information to the category of private identifiable information and thus human subjects research. For example, anonymous data on people's personal health habits becomes identifiable when linked to spatial data describing, with considerable accuracy, where a person lives. Such precise spatial data, coupled with other demographic descriptors of individuals, may enable an intruder to deductively identify individuals. This is a changed circumstance produced by major advances in observation technology and the capacity to record and store such information. Until recently, locational mapping, aerial photography, and other mechanisms to depict spatial relations were not sophisticated enough to yield private identifiable information and thus were outside the definition of human subjects research. The same transformation has occurred in the context of individual observation in public places where note-taking has been replaced by audio or video recording, and the potential identifiability of recorded data in public places can make research previously considered outside the definition fall under the scope of human subjects research.

It might be expected that the capacity to make refined measurements would lead data providers and secondary users to seek to have access to these data. Secondary use of datasets that are not identifiable and are available for public use have less scientific potential but do not create the same concerns about disclosure risk. Secondary analysts need to weigh what forms of data meet their needs and what benefits to research may be lost without the use of more precise locational information.[21]

Many of the sophisticated techniques that have been employed to preserve and optimize the analytical value of data to secondary users can be generalized to social and spatial data. Data releases can vary depending on the needs of the secondary users. For highly qualified secondary users, the use of enclaves, licensing, and other related mechanisms, as described by Rodgers and Nolte (2006), can enable the secondary user to enjoy the same richness and usefulness that was available to the primary data user. Alternatively, judicious decisions by a disclosure review committee may result in the use of techniques, such as data swapping and suppression of geographic detail, and render the data appropriate for broader dissemination to secondary users (see, for example, O'Rourke et al., 2006).

Ethical responsibilities follow for researchers engaged in data collection or the analysis of data in which information is identifiable. Ethical research *with* known human subjects requires that they be aware of and informed about the research, that they agree to participate in it, that their information be treated in confidence, and that there be benefits to the work that outweigh the risks of harm. With known persons, researchers have fiduciary obligations to these individuals as part of the compact of their participation. If secondary analysts are studying data that are similarly identifiable, they also have the same obligation to honor agreements that have been previously made.

Topics of Research

Topics of inquiry vary in sensitivity and the likelihood that research participants may believe that they are sharing information that is highly personal and private. There are individual differences among participants as to their boundaries of privacy and what they are willing to share with researchers. These differences are exacerbated when it is not only the primary researcher but also others, later, who may gain access to individuals who are seeking to keep private their status, condition, or personal information. Individual differences in people's desire to control who has access to them and to information about them are likely to arise in some of the kinds of research that include spatial linkages to social data. For example, research on domestic violence, crime, stigmatized diseases, and natural disasters would be enhanced by geographic display of incidence data. Many persons in these circumstances are quite willing to participate in research and view quite favorably the opportunity to speak to a researcher or be part of a larger enterprise. Others, however, who have been traumatized, perhaps repeatedly, are likely be highly sensitive to and fearful of invasion of their privacy and any consequent, remotely possible intrusion on their person or their social circumstances.[22]

Attention to the justness principle helps to assess whether the needs of certain populations commend the use of spatial data because of increased benefits that can derive from the research (e.g., vulnerability to toxic waste), or whether certain populations may be more vulnerable to being studied and to researchers seeking access to personal information (i.e., inequitable burden). Linked social-spatial data could add to knowledge on very personal, yet highly important topics (e.g., studying the relationship between health risks and access to health resources) that research participants and the larger society would value. Alternatively, such data could increase the vulnerability of already vulnerable populations to stigma or other forms of harm (e.g., studying drug use patterns proximal to high-crime "hot spots"). The key ethical questions include: To what extent does linking social and spatial data add to the importance of the research? To what extent does it add to the risk of disclosing personal information? How will the researcher or secondary analyst explain the benefits of the study and the value of social and spatial links to research participants and to the larger society?[23]

Consent and Confidentiality Agreements

Informed consent of research participants is the standard ethical requirement for human subjects research. Researchers have an ethical responsibility to show respect for persons and earn their trust based on the assumption that people have agreed to participate on a voluntary basis and with sufficient information and understanding to make a decision. As specified in the Belmont principles, the standard is one of subjects' having "sufficient" information. The principles allow for incomplete information in certain circumstances to ensure the validity of the research as long as the risk is minimal and the information being withheld does not pertain to risk. Typically, as part of the compact between researcher and research participant, consent to participate also includes an agreement to treat information as confidential and to ensure that no personal identifiers would disclose either subjects' participation in the research or information about them.[24] The addition of fine-grained spatial data makes implementing this promise an additional challenge.[25]

In making determinations about consent, the nature of consent, and whether to seek a waiver of consent under the federal regulations,[26] researchers and others collecting highly identifiable spatial data need to assess how they will approach the process of obtaining consent and whether and under what circumstances they would seek a waiver of consent. For example, could a waiver be appropriate in a study of at-risk driving patterns using court records to identify drivers' license suspensions and home coordinate data to study car use, but in which no direct interaction with subjects is anticipated? Given the importance of ensuring persons' autonomy to participate in research and also of maximizing public trust in research, circumstances justifying waivers of consent require close scrutiny.

When spatial data are collected along with social data, it is important for researchers as well as IRBs to consider how the need for and use of coordinate data should be described in obtaining informed consent, what agreements of confidentiality should be made, and how explicit researchers should be about secondary or unanticipated use.[27] Without some explanation, it is not reasonable to expect that research subjects would understand either the potential risks or the benefits of social and spatial data. There is good general guidance in ethics codes and in recent reports on informing research participants about future data use that is equally applicable to primary researchers and data producers engaged in social and spatial research (see, e.g., National Research Council, 2005, Recommendation 14, pp. 80-81). Nevertheless, when new media and their conceivable risks are explained, it is all too easy for the researcher to assume that the potential research participant understands the terminology used to explain the technology and its risks, and it is likewise too easy for subjects to pretend to understand rather than appear uninformed. Moreover, such problems of miscommunication are likely to vary across different sectors of the subject population. Such techniques as cognitive interviewing can be usefully employed both to develop informed consent language that is understandable to the various relevant sectors of the population and as probes to evaluate comprehension by consenting individuals (Willis, 2006).

There are instances in which the consent of research subjects may not be possible for obtaining or using linked social-spatial data. Such instances are most likely to arise in the contexts of unanticipated or secondary use. Secondary analysts may seek to use social and spatial data for which there was no previous agreement about multiple research use during the original data collection. Also, primary or secondary researchers may identify a subsequent use for linked data for which recontacting research subjects to obtain consent may not be feasible—effectively making the research impossible if consent was required. In determining whether to seek waivers of consent, researchers need to weigh obligations to research subjects and to the scientific enterprise, as the Belmont principle of beneficence specifies. Under such circumstances, salient ethical questions include: Is the research of minimal risk and sufficient potential benefit to commend being pursued without consent? Will the researcher operate consistent with any prior confidentiality agreements, extrapolating to this circumstance? Can the identity of research participants and information about them be protected in light of the privacy needs that people typically have?

Benefits

In general, the benefits of social science research typically accrue to society or to people with similar conditions or circumstances to the research subjects, rather than to individual subjects. Consonant again with the principle of beneficence, research participants should be made aware of this, and also of the fact that benefits derive from the accumulation of scientific knowledge based on information that they provide or make accessible and from having that information enhanced by linking to other information. Researchers can also communicate to participants the benefits that can derive from making the information they provide available to other qualified researchers who can reexamine findings or ask new questions using the same information.[28]

The benefits of precise spatial measurements can best be understood in this context. More extensive measurement of contextual variables, such as location permits identifying and explaining patterns and differences on a group, community, or societal scale. Emphasizing these benefits does not mean that individuals do not themselves reap personal benefits commensurate with their time and engagement. Typically an aspect of ethically responsible research is to provide some tangible benefit to participants. In the case of a heath survey with precise coordinate data, it could, for example, be a handout of proximal health clinics and routes of public transportation. With unsavory or undesirable human subjects, benefits may not accrue, but neither should direct harm due to their willingness to participate, assuming they are aware of ethical and legal limits.[29]

Overall, in assessing and communicating the benefits of research, the salient ethical questions for researchers include: Are the research participants or their communities likely to benefit from more geographically explicit research? Are they likely to receive far fewer benefits if the use of geospatial data is severely restricted? Can researchers provide research participants or their communities with added benefit by adding the geographically specific information? Can the potential benefits of linking social and spatial data be reaped without research participants being exposed to undue risk of harm or disclosure? Can the researcher set forth the benefits of such data and not overpromise?

Risk, Harm, Risk Reduction and Confidentiality Protection

As with assessing benefits, the assessment of risk in social and spatial research needs to identify both general risks associated with the research and any increased harm or risk of harm due to the use of precise locational information. For all studies, there are potential risks at each stage of the research enterprise, including in the identification or specification of the sample, data collection, database construction, data analysis, dissemination of results, and data sharing. Along with the benefits that derive from using exact coordinate data is some greater risk of disclosure made possible through the use of a readily identifiable variable.

The Belmont principles appropriately emphasize the distinction between risk of harm and severity or magnitude of harm and that the "benefits [of research] are properly contrasted with harms rather than the risk of harm." Except at the extremes, determinations of level of risk and types of harm are frequently confused.[30] Social and spatial research on highly sensitive topics for which physical, psychological, legal, or economic harms are conceivable (e.g., a study of mobility patterns and self-protective behavior of abused spouses) place a higher burden on ensuring that preserved data have a very low (approaching zero) risk of disclosure and are protected by a very secure data protection plan.[31] In some instances, researchers may wish to obtain certificates of confidentiality from federal agencies to protect, to the extent possible, some forms of data from forced disclosure.[32] Much research of importance in social science is not on highly sensitive topics, and the primary risk of harm may take the form of transitory embarrassment, stress, or discomfort. Even under such circumstances, however, efforts to reduce the risk of disclosure remain important because of the ethical value placed on honoring agreements with research participants and the ethical principle of making information on participants accessible only if essential to addressing research issues.

With linked social-spatial data, there is an incremental risk of breaching confidentiality and the potential for disclosure due to the value of preserving and using precise locational information. There is an ethical obligation to minimize disclosure risk generally—even when it remains minimal. Precise coordinate data may continue to have analytic meaning for many years, but risks associated with its use may reduce over time as migration and other life course changes alter the identifiability of these data. Nevertheless, in implementing ethically responsible research and planning for access, issues for consideration include: What technical approaches can be used, and to what extent should they be used to reduce the identifiability of social and spatial data while still retaining their scientific and analytic value? What do researchers and others who produce, manage, or disseminate data need to know to minimize risk of disclosure? What forms of data protection plans and models of restricted access are most promising to maximize the use of data and to minimize dual use (that is, unanticipated and adverse use by an intruder)[33] or inadvertent disclosure? To what extent are different strategies or guidelines needed at different stages of research (e.g., strengthened certificates of confidentiality,[34] guidelines for research reporting) in order to minimize disclosure risk?

Planning and implementing ethically responsible research, whether as primary researchers or secondary users, involve addressing this spectrum of issues. These questions serve to illustrate what needs to be asked by researchers, by data providers, by funders, and ultimately by review groups like IRBs in undertaking social and spatial research. The process is much more nuanced than a simple determination of how and at what level precise coordinate data must be masked to maximally reduce identifiability and potential breaches of confidentiality. If the data can be adequately protected from intruders, if inadvertent disclosure can be sufficiently reduced, if the risk of exposure is low, and if the harms from any exposure are only of minimal or transitory impact, then the core considerations to allow for ethical use have been met. Thus, the emphasis on strong data protection plans and conditions of responsible use is as important as masking data beyond a point at which its value would be substantially compromised.

ETHICS OF DISSEMINATION, SHARING, ACCESS, AND THE CONFIDENTIALITY NEXUS

As the foregoing discussion has emphasized, ethical decision making prominently includes attention to issues of confidentiality, but ethical considerations are larger and more comprehensive than confidentiality alone.[35] Because of the considerable scientific value of using precise coordinate data by primary researchers and secondary analysts, there is an inevitable tension between data dissemination or sharing and doing so consonant with the promises made to research participants not to disclose their identities or identifiable personal information about them. What are at once sound ethical standards—maximizing scientific gains from available information and ensuring that promises of confidentiality are kept to research participants—can conflict if the advancement of one compromises the other.

Dissemination

Ethical decision making in human subjects research typically focuses on issues that relate to identifying research populations and informing them about the study, gaining their agreement to participate, and minimizing the probability of any harm or risk of harm that might occur during the conduct of the research or with information gathered through it. Ethical responsibility as it relates to other steps in the research process, in particular research reporting and dissemination, is far rarer in discussion and decision making related to human research protection. Beyond confidentiality guarantees and cautions with respect to personal identification or the identifiability of personal information, much is implied but little is elaborated on in the federal regulations. The Belmont principles and related standards provide useful guidance for greater attention to the dissemination phase.

First, the Belmont principles are explicit about the need to contribute to the larger body of knowledge. Also, they imply that fair treatment of those who participate in research includes the dissemination of results; beneficence depends in part on the dissemination of valid new knowledge. In addition, ethical standards related to reporting on research require that the data underlying results need to be presented in sufficient detail to permit readers to follow the logic of inquiry and assess the warrants underlying inferences.[36] These objectives need to be considered in the context of how information is publicly presented with linked social-spatial data.

The presentation of precise locational information can enhance contributions to knowledge, but, with locational data, the form of presentation of research results may require special measures or procedures to be as transparent as possible without risking disclosure of the identity of research participants. How will the data be presented or displayed to avert the likelihood of identifying research participants or the potential misuse of findings? How will the research methodology and design be described to allow for maximum transparency and the accumulation of knowledge but without risking inadvertent disclosure?

Depending on the precision of the locational data and the rarity of the social data that are linked, even a map display could reveal the identity of specific individuals without mention of any specific names. A study of drug users and their dispersion and density in a community may add immeasurably to knowledge of how social networks contribute to at-risk behaviors, but also published maps by household could be tantamount to published address books in certain neighborhoods. Thus, it may be necessary in presentations or published work to coarsen the displays, swap data, or extrapolate to similarly situated geographic spaces in the same or an equivalent neighborhood, or take other steps that allow for the reporting of results while preserving the confidentiality of linked social-spatial data.[37]

Sharing

Given work of the scope, size, and significance of social and spatial research, the ethics of inquiry commends data sharing on the part of primary researchers and data collectors. Like the dissemination of results, data sharing also contributes to the important Belmont principle of contributing to the accumulation of knowledge. The Belmont Report emphasizes, as an element of beneficence, the improvement of knowledge and the benefits that can accrue to society in the form of knowledge to be gained from research. Data sharing in science can be seen as a means to that end:

fundamental to science is a commitment to openness of inquiry that enables the self-correcting and cumulative advancement of knowledge.[38]

Prior to about 1975, openness regarding human subjects data was manifested by the way research methods were described and data were presented in publications; replication of results established the validity and generalizability of results.[39] In 1985, the National Research Council, under the leadership of its Committee on National Statistics, published the report *Sharing Research Data*, which was influential in its reach (National Research Council, 1985).[40] Almost immediately, the Division of Social and Economic Science at the National Science Foundation (NSF) took up the recommendations in that report and established a data archiving policy (National Science Foundation, Division of Social and Economic Science, 1986). By the late-1980s, some federal funding agencies, most notably NSF, began to encourage more formal sharing of documented data and materials in *all* areas of science.[41] By the time the National Institutes of Health (NIH) fully elaborated its policy in 2003,[42] the ethical underpinning and normative value of data sharing were quite evident both in official policy and related educative materials.[43]

Ethical conduct in research involves not only attention to the value of data sharing but also doing so consonant with confidentiality agreements. Researchers and data producers need to plan for data sharing and the forms that data sharing can take. Especially with social and spatial data and other forms of information that may be readily identifiable, primary researchers and data producers need to ensure that research subjects are *sufficiently* informed about potential use of the data and to develop data sharing plans that can reasonably be expected to protect the identities of human subjects and personal information about them. As noted earlier, even with research in which potential harms are minimal, the broader commitment of honoring confidentiality agreements with research participants looms large even if the consequences of disclosure of personal identifiable information are small. Also, the reputation of human research with the general public will greatly influence the willingness of individuals to participate in research in the future.

From the vantage of ethically responsible research, the articulation of data sharing and data protection plans appropriate to the research go hand-in-hand. With large-scale social and spatial data (including that collected at many sites or over long-periods of time), there is the potential for considerable future use. Thus, gaining the consent of research participants could readily include noting that other researchers will have an opportunity to analyze the information. If a study is on quite personal or sensitive topics, primary researchers either could explain that information provided to others would be altered in such a way that identification would be virtually impossible, or they could indicate that other researchers can have access to identifiable information only under restricted conditions in which they commit to honoring confidentiality agreements. If the researcher plans to share data through a third-party provider (e.g., a public archive), both the researcher and the provider need to anticipate whether the level and richness of the linked coordinate and social data allow for public use data files (typically limiting the detail that can be provided) or alternatively whether restricted access arrangements need to be made (e.g., licensing agreements or access at controlled sites).

There is good general guidance for investigators and for institutional review boards on specific ways to protect the privacy of human subjects and the confidentiality of the data.[44] There is need to develop and test approaches for providing access to precise coordinate data that can maximize the analytic potential of these measurements without risking the disclosure of identifiable information in primary or secondary use. Our purpose here is not to elaborate on the methodologies, the processes for sharing data (e.g., under the direct auspices of researchers, through a data archive or enclave), or even the timing of data sharing (e.g., released in waves for longitudinal study). Our aim is to underscore the ethical basis for data sharing and that data sharing and data protection can best be addressed together by researchers and by IRBs.

Access

Secondary users of public-use data or restricted data files have an ethical obligation to contribute to the advancement of knowledge in accordance with the agreements made to produce these resources. The ethical obligations of primary researchers extend to secondary analysts. Secondary analysts are reliant on the trust provided by research participants in the research enterprise, and thus the obligation of secondary analysts is not altered by the fact that they were not themselves party to any promise with the human subjects of research.

Public archives like the Inter-university Consortium for Political and Social Research (ICPSR) explicitly set forth the obligations of secondary analysts for responsible use.[45] With data that are either publicly available or available through limited or restricted forms of access, typically researchers have an ethical requirement to use data in their current form, without the integration of additional data or enhancements of other information, unless they take additional steps to assess the ethical issues related to an expansion or change. Except for data that are publicly available, this obligation also includes not otherwise sharing data with tertiary users. In social and spatial research, this guidance on secondary use is particularly important. Secondary analysts who seek to add precise coordinate information need to examine the ethical aspects as well as the feasibility of doing so responsibly, and they need to consider issues of consent. In such instances, researchers may request waivers of consent, as noted previously, in seeking IRB approval. An IRB's ethical responsibility is to assess the reasonableness of waiver requests in light of the potential risk of harm and steps that will be taken to ameliorate that risk.

Contributing to the advancement of knowledge also obligates secondary analysts to acknowledge the sources of data as part of disseminating their results. To the extent that beneficence includes both an obligation to contribute to the well-being of research participants and the larger public good, acknowledgment of the connections between the new research and the initial research helps to ensure cumulative benefits. Most ethical guidance includes secondary analysts also acknowledging any assistance that they have received from primary researchers in gaining an understanding of or access to such data.

ETHICS EDUCATION AND TRAINING FOR
SOCIAL AND SPATIAL RESEARCH

The scientific potential of linked social-spatial data and the complex issues involved in responsible social and spatial research raise questions about how best to prepare researchers, data managers, data stewards, and secondary analysts, among others, to engage in such work. Typically preparation for research of such complexity and sophistication focuses on issues of methods and measurement: At the data collection stage, research preparation tends to emphasize what information to collect and preserve and how best to ensure that different forms of data at different units of analysis can be meaningfully gathered and linked. Primary data collection includes obtaining the consent of research participants, but practices may vary widely as to whether data sharing or future use is noted as part of that process.[46] At the data management, analysis, and dissemination stages, research preparation focuses on how to store or provide access to data at varying levels of disclosure risk or turns to technical and statistical questions about how to retain scientific value without jeopardizing confidentiality agreements. These are all important issues for those engaged in producing or using linked social-spatial data, but, in these contexts, guidance is aimed at being more instructive about the requirements for use than educative about them. Attention to confidentiality, inadvertent disclosure, requirements with respect to any data enhancements or linkage are considered part of the process of providing access to data—with any heightened sensitivity to ethical issues at this stage being a secondary benefit.[47]

Ethics education and training are not an explicit component of most graduate education programs. Ethical considerations across social and behavioral science fields and specialties are generally addressed sporadically in courses or in the supervised training and mentoring that more experienced researchers provide. Scant materials are available for course or class unless one enters the specialized literature on human research ethics,[48] contributing to faculty's giving limited attention to ethical considerations as an aspect of methodology except among those with specialized interests or expertise in this subject. Added to this, the rapidly changing circumstances related to confidentiality issues due to advances in computer technology and fine-grained identifiable measurements (in areas like coordinate data or video recording) make for more questions than answers—a factor likely to further discourage curriculum development by the nonexpert. In this context, social and spatial research is no exception. [49]

In recent years, IRBs are explicitly encouraging researchers to take courses[50] (typically available on the Internet requiring approximately one hour). In the case of research to be funded by NIH, since 2000, education is a requirement of receiving NIH support.[51] IRB members are also required to undertake training to serve in this role. Further underscoring the importance of education and training, since 2005,[52] as part of their assurance of compliance with the Public Health Service's Policies on Research Misconduct, institutions have a general responsibility to foster a research environment that promotes the responsible conduct of research and research training (with training responsibilities covering human subjects and data acquisition, management, sharing, and ownership among other issues).[53] The Office of Research Integrity[54] promotes educational activities and has oversight of institutional assurances. The current emphasis on responsible research conduct as part of the regulatory clime could support a shift in attention to ethical issues if it could be meaningfully encouraged by federal agencies and meaningfully implemented by researchers and their institutions.

Research societies in the social and behavioral sciences have sought to focus greater attention on human research ethics among their members and in departments that train in their fields (see, e.g., Iutcovich, Kennedy, and Levine, 2003; Levine and Iutcovich, 2003). Sessions at annual meetings, courses, and workshops are not uncommon—although attendance is variable. Over recent years, the American Sociological Association, the American Anthropological Association, the American Educational Research Association, and the American Historical Association, among others, have included human research protection issues on the agenda of the meetings of department chairs, directors of graduate programs, or, in the case of education research, graduate school deans. The American Statistical Association has a portion of its website dedicated to information and resources on confidentiality and privacy.[55] The Social and Behavioral Science Working Group on Human Research Protection, supported under a contractual agreement with the NIH Office of Social and Behavioral Science Research, has issued educational documents, prepared course material, and convened courses at research society meetings since 2002.[56] Directed to issues of central concern to the social and behavioral sciences, these offerings focus on such core topics as consent, confidentiality, privacy, benefits and risks, and the use of public and restricted data files. Although these efforts are not specifically focused on social and spatial research or issues involved in the collection, management, and analysis of linked data by primary researchers and secondary analysts, they provide some basis for further targeted work.

As noted earlier, the goal of balancing access with the protection of confidentiality is set forth in written materials by data stewards to inform potential users.[57] Data providers (e.g., public archives or research teams providing their own direct access) also note their responsibility to train those engaged in data preparation, database management, and the review of requests for data access to avert inadvertent disclosure. Collaborative efforts across research societies and stewardship organizations could very well provide a framework for both offering high-quality education and further encouraging graduate departments to do so as an integral part of their training programs. Outreach should also include efforts directed to fields of science engaged in social and spatial research but with less experience in human research and related ethical issues.

That ethical requirements can be seen as hurdles by researchers and users is understandable given that what is required can be mechanistic in many instances or oblique as to its goals and intent. Attention is rarely focused on sensitizing researchers, database managers, or users to ethical considerations or how to weigh them in undertaking or being a part of social and spatial research. This situation is by no means unique to social and spatial research, however. Despite the expanded requirement that researchers take various online courses in human research protection to certify to IRBs that they are prepared to undertake research, there is little formal preparation in the undergraduate or graduate curriculum directed to the ethics of research and responsible research conduct.

Ethics education is often conceived as a top-down activity in which IRBs and IRB specialists educate IRB members, researchers, and students. A major deficiency of this approach is that it tends to present generalities and to overlook the commonly observed fact that the devil is in the details.[58] In the case of social and spatial research, this problem is accentuated by the fact that certain issues, such as the fineness/coarseness of the data, are a technical matter, as are various ways of intruding on the data set or protecting the data set from intrusion. Hence, it is particularly important that social-spatial data specialists are prominent in the development of ethics education in this realm, via textbook chapters, national and regional workshops, and journal articles.

FINAL THOUGHTS

This paper has sought to provide ethical guidance to those involved in producing, using, preserving, managing, and analyzing spatially linked data. Our aim was to present an overview of the ethical issues that come into play in the research process, from design through data sharing and dissemination. It is only recently that the capacity to collect precise coordinate data over many locations and points in time and to link them to social data has developed to a point that raises human subjects issues. Using the Belmont principles as a base and extrapolating from them, we have sought to examine ethical considerations and how they might be weighed here.

This paper seeks to raise issues, not only for those involved in social and spatial research, but also for those engaged in the review of it. In relation to IRBs, we recommend a highly proactive approach, since IRBs will be largely unaware of this complex new situation, and either naively overlook serious risks or, in the absence of good communication and a one-step-at-a-time approach, could introduce barriers that could unnecessarily limit such research. The opportunities for linking to important forms of data should not be avoided, for example, because they were not anticipated in advance when approval was initially sought or because the risks of harm could not be sufficiently assessed at a prior point. The IRB process allows for continuing review with provisional approval. Thus, under certain circumstances, researchers may want to provide a broad map of their work and follow up with subsequent review when it becomes germane. Documentation would grow with each new addition or use of the data, but the researcher would not need to anticipate all uses too far in advance.[59]

Data producers and users who intend to undertake research involving linked social-spatial data will need to take time early in the planning stages to begin conversations with appropriate members of their IRBs. Of course, risks will emerge that are unforeseen; hence, the conversation must include some discussion of this possibility. There must be an understanding that these risks will be discussed openly and immediately with the IRB and incorporated into the data documentation. This rapport could deter naive risk taking by researchers or risk-averse actions by the IRB.

As implied by the observations above, research protection programs at academic or research institutions need to support and encourage IRBs to function as ethically effective decision makers. Institutional programs can be established and approved that allow IRBs to avoid mechanistic application of rules and to use the flexibility accorded to them. Openness to the coordination of multisite review or to preapproval for certain types of time-sensitive data collection are just two procedures that IRBs could introduce to facilitate review of social and spatial research consonant with human research protection. An emphasis on confidentiality and data protection plans and a willingness to use waivers of consent could similarly facilitate discoveries related to geographic location while strictly adhering to minimal risk standards.

In social and spatial research and in human research more generally, IRBs and researchers, data producers, and secondary analysts would serve the advancement of knowledge and the ethical conduct of science through taking an unusually collaborative and collegial approach. Part of doing so requires essential expertise on IRBs or IRBs involving expert consultants related to the technical and ethical issues involved in social and spatial research. Representation on the IRB of scientists knowledgeable in spatial measurement, in data disclosure methods, and in approaches that can ameliorate risk would be optimal when there are sufficient numbers of relevant protocols. The promise of social and spatial research is so significant that it is incumbent on those who propose research and those reviewing it to proceed cognizant of the contribution of research participants and committed to *benefits for all.*

NOTES

1. As used here the term embraces all of the mechanisms that permit the identification of a location through latitude and longitude coordinates. The magnitude and speed of obtaining such information due to advances in remote sensing (from satellite images to high-resolution aerial photography) and global positioning systems (GPS), coupled with the growing sophistication of geographic information systems (GIS) to store and manipulate such data, have accelerated interest in research use and applications.

2. For an excellent overview of this rapidly emerging field, see National Research Council (1998).

3. To date, much of the attention on balancing data access and considerations of confidentiality has focused on federal statistical data collections, administrative records, and other public resources (see, for example, National Research Council, 2005; Lane, 2003; de Wolf, 2003). For earlier consideration of these issues, see Duncan (1993), National Research Council (1993), and U.S. General Accounting Office (2001).

4. Two important examples relate to research ethics in complex humanitarian emergencies (see National Research Council, 2002) and with victims of disasters (see Collogan, Tuma, Dolan-Sewell, Borja, and Fleischman, 2004; Collogan, Tuma, and Fleischman, 2004). For a general consideration of challenging research circumstances, see National Bioethics Advisory Commission (2001).

5. Public Law No. 104-191, 110 Stat. 1936 (1996).

6. For useful guidance, see de Wolf, Sieber, Steel, and Zarate (2006).

7. The Federal Regulations for the Protection of Human Subjects were adopted in 1991 and Subpart A (known as the Common Rule) was accepted by 17 federal agencies as policy. Only research funded by these agencies needs to be considered by an IRB at the relevant institution, but institutions under their assurance of compliance with the federal regulations (filed with the Office of Human Research Protections; available: http://www.hhs.gov/ohrp/assurances/assurances_index.html) gener-

ally require that all human research receive IRB consideration, whether or not the work is extramurally funded, or whether it is funded by federal agencies (beyond the 17 signatories) or private foundations.

8. Calls for empirical research on human research ethics have increased in recent years. There is general awareness that human research considerations are shaped by too many assumptions about research participants (see, e.g., Levine and Skedsvold, 2007). Recent reports from the National Research Council addressed to issues of data access are strong in their calls for research (see, e.g., National Research Council, 2005, 2003a). In 2006, the *Journal of Empirical Research on Human Research Ethics*, published by the University of California Press, was established to serve as a forum for empirical research on such issues.

9. Research, for example, that graphically displayed individual-level activity patterns— leaving from home to work but stopping to have coffee with friends rather than to arrive promptly for business meetings—could encroach on personal privacy and run employment risks if confidentiality were breached.

10. For brief recent histories relating to the social and behavioral sciences generally, see National Research Council (2003a); also see the section on emergence of ethical considerations and related cites in Levine and Skedsvold (2007).

11. *Respect for persons*, *risk-benefit*, and *justice* are key considerations as they relate to the autonomy of subject populations to participate in research and to ensure that their doing so is equitable in terms of inclusion as well as exclusion. For an important example of attention to ethical considerations in the conduct of research involving prisoners, see Institute of Medicine (2007). The committee undertaking this report sought to reexamine and address such important issues as what constitutes prisoner populations, whether review of research should shift from categories of research to a risk-benefit approach, and how justice might best be understood in the context of an ethical framework.

12. Private information is one of the defining characteristics of research involving human subjects at 45 CFR 46.102(f); that is, information obtained in a context in which an individual might reasonably expect that no observation or recording is taking place or information that a person would reasonably expect will not be made public *and* is individually identifiable by the researcher. Subsequently, in setting forth the criteria for IRB approval of research at 45 CFR 46.111(a)(7), the need for provisions to protect the privacy of subjects and the confidentiality of data is emphasized. Confidentiality is also explicitly mentioned in the federal regulations at 46.116(a)(7) as an element of informed consent—that is, the need for informed consent to address the extent to which the confidentiality of records identifying research participants will be maintained.

13. Privacy and confidentiality are distinct from anonymity, which generally refers to researchers retaining no record of the identity of research participants, either because unique identifiers are unknown to the researcher or they are not included as part of the data. For an accessible discussion of the distinction between privacy, confidentiality, and anonymity, see Sieber (1992:44-45). Some researchers and secondary analysts use the term "anonymization" to refer to the removal or alteration of identifiable information—although deidentification tends to be the preferred term to refer to eliminating or masking data to reduce the likelihood of potential disclosure (see National Research Council, 1993).

14. Gutmann et al. (2005:2) made this useful distinction between the identity of subjects and information about them in the context of providing spatial data for secondary analysis. For a general discussion of identity disclosure and attribute disclosure, see National Research Council (2003:23-24, 143-144).

15. Ethical considerations in biomedical and behavioral research evolved first in the context of experimental research, including in clinical medicine, which put greater emphasis on subject recruitment, consent to participate, and benefits or risks of harm due to participation than on other phases of research—including data preservation, dissemination, access, or subsequent use. The National Research Council reports (1985, 1993, 2000, 2005) on data sharing and on access to research data— in particular public data and administrative files—are an exception to the dominant attention to the data collection stage.

16. Excellent suggestions are outlined in Gutmann et al. (2005).

17. IRBs at some institutions want to review research on extant data resources that include identifiable information even if the data are made available by third-party providers who have protocols and procedures in place for approving use. If additional data are to be linked by the secondary analyst, then IRB review is required because the additional data integration (whether or not there is new primary data collection) changes the conditions of research and potentially raises new ethical considerations in relation to research participants that need to be addressed.

18. For a recent description of ways in which data enclaves and other forms of limited access data sharing can be employed to permit qualified secondary users to analyze data with strict safeguards against disclosure of confidential information, see Rodgers and Nolte (2006).

19. The scope of this paper is directed to social and spatial research directed to producing and adding to generalizable knowledge. The definition of what constitutes research covered by the Code of Federal Regulations for the Protection of Human Subjects is set forth in 45 CFR 46.102(d), "*Research* means a systematic investigation, including research development, testing and evaluation, designed to develop or contribute to generalizable knowledge. . . ."

20. According to 45 CFR 46.102(f), "Private information must be individually identifiable (i.e., the identity of the subject is or may readily be ascertained by the investigator or associated with the information) in order for obtaining the information to constitute research involving human subject."

21. Increasingly IRBs at institutions are not doing additional review of protocols for research on public use files. For an excellent example, see the website of the University of Wisconsin, Madison, IRB at http://www.grad.wisc.edu/research/compliance/humansubjects/7.existingdata.htm. More generally, see the recommendation of the National Human Research Protections Advisory Committee on public use data files at http://www.hhs.gov/ohrp/nhrpac/documents/dataltr.pdf). Two NRC reports (National Research Council, 2003, Recommendations 5.2 and 5.3; 2005, Recommendation 6) urge the exemption of secondary analysis of public use files from additional IRB review based on certification of confidentiality protection from a data provider, including federal statistical agencies. The federal regulations at 45 CFR 46.101(b)(4) define as exempt "research involving the collection or study of existing data, documents, records . . . , if these sources are publicly available or if the information is recorded by the investigator in such a manner that subjects cannot be identified, directly or through identifiers linked to the subjects."

22. Empirical research on the complexity of undertaking research in traumatic circumstances or on traumatized populations is reviewed in Newman and Kaloupek (2004) and Newman, Risch, and Kassam-Adams (2006); see also, Griffin, Resick, Waldrop, and Mechanic (2003).

23. With certain topics of research or subject populations, researchers need to take special care to conceive of the research cognizant of the perceptions of human subjects about the study and the research procedures being used. There are many

       good examples related to ethic and cultural populations and communities, including immigrant and refugee groups, in Trimble and Fisher (2006).

24.   Since spatial data with precise coordinates by definition locate persons and their communities, community consultation about the consent process and informing communities about the research and its purposes may help to work out agreements (see, e.g., Melton et al., 1988; Marshall and Rotimi, 2001).

25.   Because precise spatial data are the equivalent of personal identifiers or close proxies for them, social and spatial research that includes such measures would typically require research participant consent. Unlike the completion and return of a survey, for example, that is completed online or received in the mail, for which executing the task can be presumed to be consent, collecting coordinate data at a person's home, workplace, or health clinic and recording or linking it to survey or social data would ethically require the knowledge and agreement of the persons potentially under study.

26.   The criteria for waivers of informed consent are set forth in 45 CFR 46.116(d).

27.   An IRB is likely to expect researchers to address what information will be conveyed to research participants about spatially explicit data and how they would be combined with other information collected in the study. An IRB is most likely to expect discussion of this linkage and any risk of disclosure when locational data are being obtained as part of a primary data collection, along with survey or other social data. The actual wording of such an informed consent process and how it is understood by potential subjects would, in accordance with ethical principles, be specified by the researcher, with explanation to the IRB as to why the information and the assurances are being presented in that format, the data protection plan to be put in place, and the level of risk of harm. Survey researchers know that some wordings of warnings raise undue alarm, erode willingness to participate in research, can skew the research sample, or may be misunderstood or not even be recognized, as when research participants sign a consent form without reading it.

28.   There is some evidence that people want their data shared if it is likely to benefit society and if risk to the research participant is minimal (see, e.g., Willison, 2003).

29.   The "idealized type" of human subject is a person of value in terms of community norms of decency and trustworthiness. Like other areas of inquiry, social and spatial research may focus on undesirable or unsavory persons (for example, a study of diffusion of fraudulent medical practices among physicians). The ethical obligation to be respectful of research participants and not to increase their vulnerability is part of the consent agreement. There are limitations to agreements relating in some instances to a duty to report (e.g., learning about identifiable child abuse) that need to be made clear to human subjects as part of gaining their informed consent (see the discussion of research populations in Levine and Skedsvold, 2007).

30.   "Risk" and "harm" are terms that are often conflated (see the Risk and Harm Report of the Social and Behavioral Sciences Working Group on Human Research Protections at http://www.aera.net/aera.old/humansubjects/risk-harm.pdf). "Harm" refers to potential adverse consequences and "risk" refers to the likelihood of their occurrences. There are standards for minimal risk implied in codes of ethics and enunciated explicated in 45 CFR 46.102(i) that set forth that the "probability and magnitude of harm or discomfort anticipated in the research are not greater in and of themselves than those ordinarily encountered in daily life or during the performance of routine physical or psychological examinations or tests." While this definition offers rules of thumb, in no area does it provide the empirical clarity that would be useful (see also Wendler et al., 2005).

31. For useful general recommendations on confidentiality and research data protections, see the National Human Research Protections Advisory Committee (2002).

32. Certificates of confidentiality are issued by designated federal agencies to protect the privacy of research subjects by protecting investigators and institutions from being compelled to release information that could be used to identify subjects with a research project. They allow the investigator and others who have access to research records to refuse to disclose identifying information in any civil, criminal, administrative, legislative, or other proceeding, whether at the federal, state, or local level (see, e.g., the National Institutes of Health web site at http://grants1.nih.gov/grants/policy/coc/background.htm). For a compilation of federal research confidentiality statutes and codes prepared by the Social and Behavioral Sciences Working Group for the National Human Research Protections Advisory Committee, see http://www.aera.net/aera.old/humansubjects/NHRPAC_Final_Conf_Table.pdf.

33. Dual-use research is of major concern in the biological sciences. As defined in the National Security Advisory Board for Biosecurity Charter, dual use refers to "biological research with legitimate scientific purpose that may be misused to pose a biologic threat to public health and/or national security" (Shea, 2006:. CRS-2).

34. Certificates of confidentiality vary in their reach and protection, and the need to strengthen or align them across federal agencies is generally recognized (see National Human Research Protections Advisory Committee, 2002).

35. Fienberg (2004) makes the point that protecting confidentiality is not synonymous with ethical behavior.

36. See section 7 on ethics in reporting in American Educational Research Association, (2006).

37. Ethical decision making can require consulting with expert peers to ensure that steps are taken in publications or presentation that do not compromise research participants but do so with a presumption that openness in research dissemination is optimal for transparent and well-warranted reporting. Other areas of science also face the challenge of how to maximize openness in research reporting while remaining sensitive to potential risks of harm. Some of the current discussion in the life sciences about the reporting of results consonant with concerns about security issues is a new domain deeply engaged in trying to understand how best to balance both ethical considerations (see, e.g., Vest, 2003; Somerville and Atlas, 2005).

38. For one of the earliest and most profound statements of the norms guiding science (originally published in 1942), see Merton (1973).

39. There was some early attention in the 1970s to issues of access to government data and the conditions for dissemination of microdata sets (including attention to linkages to survey data) in a report of the American Statistical Association (1977). See also the Bellagio principles, which were developed in 1977 at a conference of academic and government representatives from five countries (Canada, the United States, the Federal Republic of Germany, Sweden, and the United Kingdom) convened to consider privacy, confidentiality, and the use of government microdata for research and statistical purposes. The principles call for expanded access to the research and statistical community and also addressed issues of data linkage consonant with confidentiality protections (see Flaherty, 1978).

40. Also for an overview of the emergence of data sharing as a practice integral to the openness of science, see Sieber (1991). In recent years, the biological sciences have also been grappling with the principles underlying the sharing of data and software as well as materials related to publication. Based on discussion at a workshop, the National Research Council Committee on Responsibilities of Authorship in the Biological Sciences articulated recommendations for sharing publication-related prod-

ucts that are familiar in tone and substance to those specified in the social and behavioral sciences (see National Research Council, 2003b).

41. The National Science Foundation first specified a data sharing requirement agency-wide in April 1989. The current statement of NSF policy on Dissemination and Sharing of Research Results (section 734) is in the Grant Policy Manual at http://www.nsf.gov/pubs/manuals/gpm05_131/gpm05_131.pdf.

42. NIH issued Data Sharing Policy and Implementation Guidelines for grants of $500,000 or more annually in direct costs, which is available: http://grants.nih.gov/grants/policy/data_sharing/data_sharing_guidance.htm.

43. See, e.g., Frequently Asked Questions at http://grants1.nih.gov/grants/policy/data_sharing/data_sharing_faqs.htm; Data Sharing Workbook at http://grants1.nih.gov/grants/policy/data_sharing/data_sharing_workbook.pdf; Data Sharing Regulations/Policy/Guidance Chart for NIH Awards at http://grants1.nih.gov/grants/policy/data_sharing/data_sharing_chart%20.doc; Data Sharing Brochure at http://grants1.nih.gov/grants/policy/data_sharing/data_sharing_brochure.pdf.

44. Helpful guidance is provided in Duncan (2003); see also O'Rourke et al. (2006). In addition, *Expanding Access to Research Data: Reconciling Risks and Opportunities* (National Research Council, 2005) specifically addresses a range of approaches to allowing greater access to federally collected data while strengthening confidentiality protections. The NIH documents also provide useful elaboration on considerations that can guide the development of data access and data sharing plans.

45. See, e.g., the ICPSR Responsible Use Statement at http://www.icpsr.umich.edu/org/policies/respuse.html.

46. Practices are changing as federal funding agencies like NIH are more explicit about data sharing and the need to address data sharing or future use as part of the process of obtaining informed consent. See the National Institutes of Health Data Sharing Policy and Implementation Guidelines at http://grants.nih.gov/grants/policy/data_sharing/data_sharing_guidance.htm.

47. The National Longitudinal Study of Adolescent Health (Add Health) is a good example of a major nationally representative longitudinal study that provides potential users with straightforward information on available public-use data sets and restricted-use data sets, with spatial analysis data being available through restricted use. Access to restricted use data requires an IRB-approved security plan and agreement to a data-use contract (Requirements for access to Restricted-Use Contractual Data are described at http://www.cpc.unc.edu/projects/addhealth/data/restricteduse.) Educative guidance of steps to avert deductive disclosure is provided on the Add Health website at http://www.cpc.unc.edu/projects/addhealth/data/dedisclosure. The Project on Human Development in Chicago Neighborhoods, also a major longitudinal, multimethod study, has public-use files and restricted data available through the Inter-university Consortium for Political and Social Research. Precise locational data are considered sensitive information and obtainable through ICPSR's restricted-use agreement or secure data enclave (see http://www.icpsr.umich.edu/PHDCN/about.html).

48. Exceptions include National Research Council (2003, 2005), which could be adopted in course and class. Also, for useful background texts, see Sieber (1992) and Fisher (2003).

49. The Center for Spatially Integrated Social Science (CSISS) at the University of California, Santa Barbara undertakes a valuable range of activities to foster capacity building in researchers, including workshops, extensive bibliographic references, course syllabi, information on best practices, and so forth (see http://www.csiss.org/). The syllabi included on the website for courses taught on spatial analysis at different

institutions make no mention of ethical considerations. The CSISS also produced a very informative best practices volume in 2004 (Goodchild and Janelle, 2004). This book is directed to the potential value of thinking spatially and sets forth examples of spatial analysis, but there was no attention to ethical considerations for potential researchers or data analysts.

50. The University of Chicago Social and Behavioral Sciences IRB emphasizes education and provides useful educational resources (see http://humansubjects.uchicago.edu/sbsirb/education.html). Also, its *IRB & Investigator Manual* (see http://human subjects.uchicago.edu/sbsirb/manual/sbsirb_manual.pdf) is a very helpful document for both those preparing research and reviewing protocols.

51. Effective October 2000, NIH requires education on the protection of human research participants for all investigators submitting applications for research involving human subjects under contracts or awards. See Required Education in the Protection of Human Research Participants at http://grants.nih.gov/grants/guide/notice-files/NOT-OD-00-039.html; also see Frequently Asked Questions for the Requirement for Education on the Protection of Human Subjects at http://grants.nih.gov/grants/policy/hs_educ_faq.htm. Although a good deal of information is offered on the website, the number and range of opportunities for training are quite limited, in particular for research grounded in the social and behavioral sciences.

52. See Public Health Service Policies on Research Misconduct, 42CFR Parts 50 and 93, at http://ori.dhhs.gov/documents/42_cfr_parts_50_and_93_2005.pdf.

53. Training in the responsible conduct of research was an element of National Research Service Award (NRSA) institutional research training grants (T32) prior to 2005, but attention to research conduct as part of institutional assurances heightened attention to this component: "Every predoctoral and postdoctoral NRSA trainee supported by an institutional research training grant must receive instruction in the responsible conduct of research. (For more information on this provision, see the NIH Guide for Grants and Contracts, Volume 21, Number 43, November 27, 1992, available: http://grants.nih.gov/grants/guide/notice-files/not92-236.html.) Applications must include a description of a program to provide formal or informal instruction in scientific integrity or the responsible conduct of research. . . ."

54. The mission of the Office of Research Integrity is to monitor institutions' investigations of research misconduct and promote the responsible conduct of research through education, prevention, and regulatory activities (see http://ori.dhhs.gov/).

55. This portion of the website is operated by the Committee on Privacy and Confidentiality of the American Statistical Association; see http://www.amstat.org/comm/cmtepc/index.cfm?fuseaction=main.

56. For further information on the working group and its educational activities, see http://www.aera.net/Default.aspx?id=669.

57. Organizations that serve as archives for data resources and stewards providing access for their use offer materials that serve to educate and inform researchers and secondary analysts about the ethical as well as technical issues involved in sharing and gaining access to data (see, e.g., ICPSR Responsible Use Statement at http://www.icpsr.umich.edu/org/policies/respuse.html). Also, the Henry A. Murray Research Archive of the Harvard-MIT Data Center is the repository for qualitative and quantitative research data at the Institute for Quantitative Social Science. It has materials on data archiving that offer brief guidance, from data collection through transfer to an archive, and on steps to facilitate data sharing (see http://murray.harvard.edu/mra/service.jsp?id=55&bct=dData%252BPreservation.p5.s55) or application for data use (see http://www.murray.harvard.edu/mra/showcontent.jsp?key=DATA_APPLICATION_FORM). The guidance sets forth conditions for use of various forms of data, including video and audio recordings.

58. One useful example of an accessible educative document is U.S. General Accounting Office (2001).
59. A similar approach was discussed by F.J. Levine regarding natural and humanitarian disasters and strategies for ongoing flexible review processes (see National Research Council, 2002).

REFERENCES

American Anthropological Association
    1998   *Code of Ethics.* Arlington, VA: American Anthropological Association.
American Association for Public Opinion Research
    2003   Protection of Human Participants in Survey Research: A Source Document for Institutional Review Boards. Available: http://www.aapor.org/default.asp?page=news_and_issues/aapor_statement_for_irb. [accessed November 25, 2005].
    2005   Code of Professional Ethics and Practices. Available: http://www.aapor.org/pdfs/AAPOR_Code_2005.pdf [accessed November 25, 2005].
American Educational Research Association
    2006   Standards for reporting on empirical social science research in AERA publications. *Educational Researcher* 35(6):33-40.
American Political Science Association
    1998   *A Guide to Professional Ethics in Political Science.* Washington, DC: American Political Science Association.
American Psychological Association
    2003   Ethical principles of psychologists and code of conduct. *American Psychologist* 57:1060-1073.
American Sociological Association
    1997   *Code of Ethics.* Washington, DC: American Sociological Association.
American Statistical Association
    1977   Report of ad hoc committee on privacy and confidentiality. *The American Statistician* 31(2):59-78.
    1999   *Ethical Guidelines for Statistical Practice.* Alexandria, VA: Author.
Armstrong, M.P., G. Rushton, and D.L. Zimmerman
    1999   Geographic masking health data to preserve confidentiality. *Statistics in Medicine* 18:497-525.
Association of American Geographers
    1998   Statement on Professional Ethics. Available: http://www.aag.org/publications/other%20pubs/ethicsstatement.html [accessed November 25, 2005].
Collogan, L.K., F. Tuma, R. Dolan-Sewell, S. Borja, and A.R. Fleischman
    2004   Ethical issues pertaining to research in the aftermath of disaster. *Journal of Traumatic Stress* 17:363-372.
Collogan, L.K., F.K. Tuma, and A.R. Fleischman
    2004   Research with victims of disaster: Institutional review board considerations. *IRB: Ethics & Human Research* 26(July-August):9-11.
de Wolf, V.A.
    2003   Issues in accessing and sharing confidential survey and social science data. *Data Science Journal* 2:66-74.
de Wolf, V.A., J.E. Sieber, P.M. Steel, and A.O. Zarate
    2006   Part II: HIPAA and disclosure risk. *IRB: Ethics & Human Research*, 28(January-February), 6-11.

Duncan, G.T.
    1993   Special issue on confidentiality and data access. *Journal of Official Statistics* 93:269-607.
    2003   Confidentiality and data access issues for institutional review boards. Pp. 235-247 in National Research Council, *Protecting Participants and Facilitating Social and Behavioral Sciences Research*. C.F. Citro, D.R. Ilgen, and C. B. Marrett, eds. Panel on Institutional Review Boards, Surveys, and Social Science Research. Washington, DC: The National Academies Press.
Fienberg, S.E.
    2004   Confidentiality in Geo-Spatially-Linked Data: How Robust Are the Solutions? Presentation at the Workshop on Confidentiality Issues in Linking Geographically Explicit and Self-Identifying Data, The National Academies, Washington, DC, December 9-10.
Fisher, C.B.
    2003   *Decoding the Ethics Code: A Practical Guide for Psychologists*. Thousand Oaks, CA: Sage Publications.
Flaherty, D.H.
    1978   Report of the Bellagio conference. *Journal of the Royal Statistical Society. Series A (General)* 141:401-405.
Golden, M.L., R.R. Downs, and K. Davis-Packard
    2005   Confidentiality Issues and Policies Related to the Utilization and Dissemination of Geospatial Data for Public Health Applications. A report to the Public Health Applications of Earth Science Program, National Aeronautics and Space Administration, Science Mission Directorate, Applied Sciences Program. Prepared by the Socioeconomic Data and Applications Center, Center for International Earth Science Information Network, Columbia University, March 2005. Available: http://www.ciesin.columbia.edu/pdf/SEDAC_ConfidentialityReport.pdf [accessed November 25, 2005].
Goodchild, M.F., and D.G. Janelle, eds.
    2004   *Spatially Integrated Social Science*. New York: Oxford University Press.
Griffin, M.G., P.A. Resick, A.E. Waldrop, and M.B. Mechanic
    2003   Participation in trauma research: Is there evidence of harm? *Journal of Traumatic Stress* 16:221-227.
Gutmann, M., K. Witkowski, C. Colyer, J.M. O'Rourke, and J. McNally
    2005   Providing Spatial Data for Secondary Analysis: Issues and Current Practices Relating to Confidentiality. Unpublished manuscript, Inter-university Consortium for Political and Social Research, University of Michigan (available from Myron Gutmann).
Institute of Medicine
    2007   *Ethical Considerations for Research Involving Prisoners*. Committee on Ethical Considerations for Revisions to DHHS Regulations for Protection of Prisoners Involved in Research, L.O. Gostin, C. Vanchieri, and A. Pope eds. Washington, DC: The National Academies Press.
Iutcovich, J.M., J.M. Kennedy, and F.J. Levine
    2003   Establishing an ethical climate in support of research integrity: Efforts and activities of the American Sociological Association. *Science and Engineering Ethics* 9:201-205.
Kwan, M.P., I. Casas, and B.C. Schmitz
    2004   Protection of geoprivacy and accuracy of spatial information: How effective are geographical masks? *Cartographica* 39:15-28.

Kwan, M.R., and J. Lee
    2004   Geovisualization of human activity patterns using 3D GIS. Pp. 18-66 in M.F. Goodchild and D.G. Janelle, eds., *Spatially Integrated Social Science*. New York: Oxford University Press.

Lane, J.
    2003   Key Issues in Confidentiality Research: Results of an NSF Workshop. Available: http://www.nsf.gov/sbe/ses/mms/nsfworkshop_summary1.pdf [accessed November 25, 2005].

Levine, F.J., and J.M. Iutcovich
    2003   Challenges in studying the effects of scientific societies on research integrity. *Science and Engineering Ethics* 9:257-268.

Levine, F.J., and P.R. Skedsvold
    2007   Behavioral and social science research. In E.J. Emmanuel, R.A. Crouch, C. Grady, R. Lie, F. Miller, and D. Wendler (Eds.) *The Oxford Textbook of Clinical Research Ethics*. Oxford, England: Oxford University Press.

Marshall, P.A., and C. Rotimi
    2001   Ethical challenges in community-based research. *American Journal of the Medical Sciences* 322(5):241-245.

Melton, G.B., R.J. Levine, G.P., Kocher, R Rosenthal, and W.C. Thompson
    1988   Community consultation in socially sensitive research: Lessons from clinical trials on treatments for AIDS. *American Psychologist* 43:573-581.

Merton, R.K.
    1973   The normative structure of science. In R.K. Merton, ed., *The Sociology of Science: Theoretical and Empirical Investigations*. Chicago, IL: University of Chicago Press.

National Bioethics Advisory Commission
    2001   *Ethical and Policy Issues in Research Involving Human Participants: Vols I, II*. Bethesda, MD: National Bioethics Advisory Commission.

National Commission for the Protection of Human Subjects of Biomedical and Behavioral Research
    1979   *Belmont Report: Ethical Principles and Guidelines for the Protection of Human Subjects of Research*. (GPO No. 887-809). Washington, DC: U.S. Government Printing Office. Also available: http://ohsr.od.nih.gov/guidelines/belmont.html [accessed November 13, 2005].

National Human Research Protections Advisory Committee
    2002   Recommendations on Confidentiality and Research Data Protections. Available: http://www.aera.net/aera.old/humansubjects/NHRPAC_Final_Confidentiality.pdf.

National Research Council
    1985   *Sharing Research Data*. Committee on National Statistics, S.E. Fienberg, M.M. Martin, and M.L. Straf, eds. Washington, DC: National Academy Press.
    1993   *Private Lives and Public Policies: Confidentiality and Accessibility of Government Statistics*. Committee on National Statistics, G.T. Duncan, T.B. Jabine, and V.A. de Wolf, eds. Washington, DC: National Academy Press.
    1998   *People and Pixels: Linking Remote Sensing and Social Science*. Committee on the Human Dimensions of Global Change, D. Liverman, E.F. Moran, R.R. Rindfuss, and P.C. Stern, eds. Washington, DC: National Academy Press.
    2000   *Improving Access to and Confidentiality of Research Data: Report of a Workshop*. Committee on National Statistics, C. Mackie and N. Bradburn, eds. Washington, DC: National Academy Press.

2002   *Research Ethics in Complex Humanitarian Emergencies: Summary of a Work-shop.* H, Reed, Rapporteur, Roundtable on the Demography of Forced Migra-tion, Committee on Population. Division of Behavioral and Social Sciences and Education. Washington, DC: The National Academies Press.

2003a   *Protecting Participants and Facilitating Social and Behavioral Sciences Research.* Panel on Institutional Review Boards, Surveys, and Social Science Research, C.F. Citro, D.R. Ilgen, and C.B. Marrett, eds.. Washington, DC: The National Acad-emies Press.

2003b   *Sharing Publication-Related Data and Materials.* Committee on Responsibilities of Authorship in the Life Sciences. Washington, DC: The National Academies Press.

2005   *Expanding Access to Research Data; Reconciling Risks and Opportunities.* Panel on Data Access for Research Purposes, Committee on National Statistics. Wash-ington, DC: The National Academies Press.

National Science Foundation, Division of Social and Economic Science
1986   Data Archiving Policy and Implementation Guidance. Materials available from F.J. Levine at flevine@aera.net.

Newman, E., and D.G. Kaloupek
2004   The risks and benefits of participating in trauma-focused research studies. *Jour-nal of Traumatic Stress* 17:383-394.

Newman, E., E. Risch, and N. Kassam-Adams
2006   Ethical issues in trauma-related research: A review. *Journal of Empirical Re-search on Human Research Ethics* 1(3):29-46.

O'Rourke, J., S. Roehrig, S. Heeringa, B. Reed, W. Birdsall, M. Overcashier, M., and K. Zidar
2006   Solving problems of disclosure risk while retaining key analytic uses of publicly released microdata. *Journal of Empirical Research on Human Research Ethics* 1(3):63-84.

Rindfuss, R.R., and P.C. Stern
1998   Linking remote sensing and social science: The need and the challenges. Pp. 1-27 in National Research Council, *People and Pixels: Linking Remote Sensing and Social Science.* Committee on the Human Dimensions of Global Change, D. Liverman, E.F. Moran, R.R. Rindfuss and P.C. Stern, eds. Washington, DC: National Academy Press.

Rodgers, W., and M. Nolte
2006   Disclosure review procedures in an academic setting: Example of the Health and Retirement Study. *Journal of Empirical Research on Human Research Ethics* 1(3):85-98.

Shea, D.A.
2006   *Oversight of Dual-Use Biological Research: The National Science Advisory Board for Biosecurity.* (CRS Report No. RL33342). Washington, DC: Congres-sional Research Service.

Sieber, J.E.
1991   Introduction: Sharing social science data. In J.E. Sieber (Ed.), *Sharing Social Science Data: Advantages and Challenges.* Newbury Park, CA: Sage Publica-tions.

1992   *Planning Ethically Responsible Research: A Guide for Students and Internal Review Boards.* Newbury Park, CA: Sage Publications.

Somerville, M.A., and R.M. Atlas
2005   Ethics: A weapon to counter bioterrorism. *Science* 307:1881-1882.

Trimble, J.E., and C.B. Fisher
    2006   *The Handbook of Ethical Research with Ethnocultural Populations and Communities*, Thousand Oaks, CA: Sage Publications.
Urban and Regional Information Systems Association
    2003   A GIS Code of Ethics. Available: http://www.urisa.org/ethics/code_of_ethics.htm [accessed August 9, 2005].
U.S. General Accounting Office
    2001   *Record Linkage and Privacy: Issues in Creating New Federal Research and Statistical Information.* (GAO-01-126SP). Washington, DC: U.S. General Accounting Office.
VanWey, L.K., R.R. Rindfuss, M.P. Gutmann, B.E. Entwisle, and D.L. Balk
    2005   Confidentiality and spatially explicit data: Concerns and challenges. *Proceedings of the National Academy of Sciences* 102:15337-15342.
Vest, C.M.
    2003   Balancing security and openness in research and education. *Academe.* Available: http://www.aaup.org/publications/Academe/2003/03so/03sowest.htm [accessed January 7, 2006].
Wendler, D., L. Belsky, K.M. Thompson, and E.J. Emanuel
    2005   Quantifying the federal minimal risk standard: Implications for pediatric research without a prospect of direct benefit. *Journal of the American Medical Association* 294:826-832.
Willis, G.
    2006   Cognitive interviewing as a tool for improving the informed consent process. *Journal of Empirical Research on Human Research Ethics* 1(1):9-23.
Willison, D.J.
    2003   Privacy and the secondary use of data for health research. Experience in Canada, and suggested directions forward. *Journal of Health Services Research and Policy* 8(Suppl 1):17-23.

Biographical Sketches for Panel Members and Staff

Myron P. Gutmann (*Chair*) is a professor of history and director of the Inter-university Consortium for Political and Social Research (ICPSR) at the University of Michigan. Prior to joining the Michigan faculty in August of 2001, he was a professor of history and geography and director of the Population Research Center at the University of Texas at Austin. His research covers interdisciplinary historical topics, especially in health, population, economy, and the environment, and he has used a variety of approaches to study population-land use interactions. He also does research and writes on issues relating to data preservation and dissemination and about confidentiality protection in data used for secondary analysis. He is the author of *War and Rural Life in the Early Modern Low Countries*, and *Toward the Modern Economy, Early Industry in Europe, 1500-1800*, as well as more than 50 articles and chapters. He has been a member of the National Academies' Committee on the Human Dimensions of Global Change and its Panel on New Research in Population and Environment, as well as other national advisory committees and editorial boards. Gutmann received a B.A. from Columbia University, an M.A. from Princeton University, and a Ph.D. in history from Princeton University.

Marc P. Armstrong is a professor and chair of the Department of Geography at The University of Iowa, where he also holds an appointment in the Graduate Program in Applied Mathematical and Computational Sciences. A primary focus of his research is on the use of parallel processing to improve the performance of analysis methods used in spatial decision support systems. Other research interests are in mobile computing, privacy aspects of geospatial technologies, and evolutionary computation. He has served as North American editor of the *International Journal of Geographical Information Science* and on the editorial boards of many other journals. He has published more than 100 papers in a wide variety of academic journals, including the *Annals of the Association of American Geographers*, *Statistics and Medicine*, *Mathematical Geology*, and *Journal of the American Society for Information Science*. He received a Ph.D. from the University of Illinois at Urbana-Champaign.

Deborah Balk is associate professor at the Baruch School of Public Affairs and acting associate director of the Institute for Demographic Research at the City University of New York. Previously, she was a research scientist at the Center for International Earth Science Information Network at Columbia University, where she was also the lead project scientist for the Socioeconomic Data and Applications Center, working on large-scale data integration of geographic, survey, and administrative data. Among her current projects, she is the principal investigator on two studies of urbanization and one on emerging infectious disease. She is a member of the Working Group on Urbanisation of the International Union for the Scientific Study of Population. She received a B.A. and M.A. from the University of Michigan-Ann Arbor and a Ph.D. in demography from the University of California at Berkeley.

Kathleen (Kass) O'Neill Green recently retired from her position as president of Space Imaging Solutions, a division of Space Imaging, LLC. While with Space Imaging, she directed programs that offered satellite imagery, remote sensing, and GIS (global information services) services to clients worldwide. She currently serves as an independent consultant and board member to public, private, and nonprofit natural resource and geospatial organizations. Her background includes 30 years of experience in natural resource policy, economics, GIS analysis, and remote sensing. She is the author of numerous articles on GIS and remote sensing and coauthored a book on the practical aspects of accuracy assessment. She is the recent past president of Management Association for Private Photogrammetric Surveyors (MAPPS), an organization of private mapping firms dedicated to advancing the mapping industry. She received a B.S. in forestry and resource management from the University of California at Berkeley and an M.S. in resource policy and management from the University of Michigan-Ann Arbor.

Felice J. Levine is executive director of the American Educational Research Association (AERA). Previously, she served as executive officer of the American Sociological Association, as a program director at the National

Science Foundation, and as senior research social scientist at the American Bar Foundation. Her work has concentrated on science policy issues, including research ethics, data access and sharing, and peer review; academic and scientific professions; and diversity in higher education. She was a member of the National Human Research Protections Advisory Committee of the U.S. Department of Health and Human Services and on the advisory committee for the decennial census. She is currently on the executive committee of the Consortium of Social Science Associations and served as its chair from 1997 to 2000 and is on the Board of Directors of the Council of Professional Associations on Federal Statistics. She is a fellow of the American Psychological Society and of the American Association for the Advancement of Science. She holds A.B., A.M. and Ph.D. degrees in sociology and psychology from the University of Chicago.

Harlan Onsrud is a professor in the Department of Spatial Information Science and Engineering at the University of Maine. His research focuses on the analysis of legal, ethical, and institutional issues that affect the creation and use of digital databases and the assessment of the social effects of spatial technologies. He is president elect of the Global Spatial Data Infrastructure Association (GSDI), past president of the University Consortium for Geographic Information Science (UCGIS), and past chair of the U.S. National Committee (USNC) on Data for Science and Technology (CODATA) of the National Research Council. He is a licensed engineer, land surveyor, and attorney. Current and past research projects have been funded by the National Science Foundation, the National Geospatial-Intelligence Agency, the Federal Geographic Data Committee, and the U.S. Department of Education. He holds B.S. and M.S. degrees in engineering and a J.D., all from the University of Wisconsin.

Jerome P. Reiter is an assistant professor at the Institute of Statistics and Decision Sciences at Duke University. His primary research areas include statistical methods for preserving data confidentiality, handling missing data, and making casual inference. He works extensively with the U.S. Census Bureau and the National Institute of Statistical Science on research in statistical disclosure limitation. He is a member of the committee on Privacy and Confidentiality of the American Statistical Association. He serves on the editorial board of the *Journal of the American Statistical Association*, the *Journal of Privacy and Confidentiality*, and *Survey Methodology*. He received a B.S. in mathematics from Duke University and a Ph.D. in statistics from Harvard University.

Ronald Rindfuss is the Robert Paul Ziff distinguished professor of sociology and a fellow at the Carolina Population Center (CPC) at the University of North Carolina-Chapel Hill and a senior fellow at the East-West Center in Honolulu. He previously served as director of the CPC. As a social demographer, his work focuses on the timing and sequencing of cohabitation, marriage, childbearing, divorce, education, migration, and employment. He is currently working on the relationship between population processes and the environment, examining migration and social change in Thailand examining the consequences of child care patterns in Norway and examining changes in family processes in Japan. He is a past president of the Population Association of America and a fellow of the American Association for the Advancement of Science. He holds a B.A. from Fordham University and a Ph.D. from Princeton University, both in sociology.

Paul C. Stern (*Study Director*) is a senior staff officer at the National Research Council and study director of the Committee on the Human Dimensions of Global Change. His research interests include the determinants of environmentally significant behavior, particularly at the individual level; participatory processes for informing environmental decision making; and the governance of environmental resources and risks. He is the coeditor of numerous National Research Council publications, including *Population, Land Use, and Environment: Research Directions* (2005), *The Drama of the Commons* (2002), and *People and Pixels: Linking Remote Sensing and Social Science* (1998). He is a fellow of the American Association for the Advancement of Science and the American Psychological Association. He holds a B.A. from Amherst College and an M.A. and Ph.D. from Clark University, all in psychology.